THE

War Powers of the President,

AND THE

LEGISLATIVE POWERS OF CONGRESS

IN RELATION TO

Rebellion, Treason and Slavery.

BY WILLIAM WHITING.

BOSTON.
JOHN L. SHOREY,
13 WASHINGTON STREET.
1862.

CONSTITUTION

OF THE

UNITED STATES OF AMERICA.

INTRODUCTION.

THE PURPOSE FOR WHICH IT WAS FOUNDED.

The Constitution of the United States, as declared in the preamble, was ordained and established by the people, "in order to form a more perfect union, establish justice, insure domestic tranquillity, provide for the common defence, promote the general welfare, and secure the blessings of liberty to themselves and their posterity."

HOW IT HAS BEEN VIOLATED.

A handful of slave-masters have broken up that Union, have overthrown justice, and have destroyed domestic tranquillity. Instead of contributing to the common defence and public welfare, or securing the blessings of liberty to themselves and their posterity, they have waged war upon their country, and have attempted to establish, over the ruins of the Republic, an aristocratic government founded upon Slavery.

"THE INSTITUTION" *vs.* THE CONSTITUTION.

It is the conviction of many thoughtful persons, that slavery has now become practically irreconcilable with republican institutions, and that it constitutes, at the present time, the chief obstacle to the restoration of the Union. They know that slavery can triumph only by overthrowing the republic; they believe that the republic can triumph only by overthrowing slavery.

"THE PRIVILEGED CLASS."

Slaveholding communities constitute the only "*privileged class*" of persons who have been admitted into the Union. They alone have the right to vote for their *property* as well as for themselves. In the free States citizens vote only for themselves. The former are allowed to count, as part of their representative numbers, three fifths of all slaves. If this privilege, which was accorded only to the original States, had not been extended (contrary, as many jurists contend, to the true intent and meaning of the constitution) so as to include other States subsequently formed, the stability of government would not have been seriously endangered by the temporary toleration of this "institution," although it was inconsistent with the principles which that instrument embodied, and revolting to the sentiments cherished by a people who had issued to the world the Declaration of Independence, and had fought through the revolutionary war to vindicate and maintain the rights of man.

UNEXPECTED GROWTH OF SLAVERY.

The system of involuntary servitude, which had received, as it merited, the general condemnation of the leading southern and northern statesmen of the country, — of those who were most familiar with its evils, and of all fair-minded persons throughout the world, — seemed, at the time when our government was founded, about to vanish and disappear from this continent, when the spinning jenny of Crompton, the loom of Wyatt, the cotton gin of Whitney, and the manufacturing capital of England, combined to create a new and unlimited demand for that which is now the chief product of southern agriculture. Suddenly, as if by magic, the smouldering embers of slavery were rekindled, and its flames, like autumnal fires upon the prairies, have rapidly swept over and desolated the southern states; and, as that local, domestic institution, which seemed so likely to pass into an ignominious and unlamented grave, has risen to claim an unbounded empire, hence the present generation is called upon to solve questions and encounter dangers not foreseen by our forefathers.

SLAVERY ABOLISHED BY EUROPEAN GOVERNMENTS.

In other countries the scene has been reversed. France, with unselfish patriotism, abolished slavery in 1794; and though Napoleon afterwards reëstablished servitude in most of the colonies, it was finally abolished in 1848. England has merited and received her highest tribute of honor from the enlightened nations of the world for that great act of Parliament in 1833, whereby she proclaimed universal emancipation.

In 1844, King Oscar informed the Swedish states of his desire to do away with involuntary servitude in his dominions; in 1846 the legislature provided the pecuniary means for carrying that measure into effect; and now all the slaves have become freemen.

Charles VIII., King of Denmark, celebrated the anniversary of the birth of the Queen Dowager by abolishing slavery in his dependencies, on the 28th of July, 1847.

In 1862, Russia has consummated the last and grandest act of emancipation of modern times.

While Europe has thus practically approved of the leading principle of the American constitution, as founded on justice, and as essential to public welfare, the United States, as represented by the more recent administrations, have practically repudiated and abandoned it. Europe, embarrassed by conservative and monarchical institutions, adopts the preamble to that instrument, as a just exposition of the true objects for which governments should be established, and accordingly abolishes slavery — while, in this country, in the mean time, slavery, having grown strong, seeks by open rebellion to break up the Union, and to abolish republican democracy. [Note A.]

SLAVERY IN 1862 NOT SLAVERY IN 1788.

However harmless that institution may have been in 1788, it is now believed by many, that, with few but honorable exceptions, the *slave-masters* of the present day, *the privileged class*, cannot, or will not, conduct themselves so as to render it longer possible, by peaceable association with them, to preserve "the Union," to "establish justice," "insure domestic tranquillity, the general welfare, the common defence, or the blessings of liberty to ourselves or our posterity." And since the wide-spread but secret conspiracies of traitors in the slave states for the last thirty years; their hatred of the Union, and determination to destroy it; their abhorrence of republican institutions, and of democratic government; their preference for an "oligarchy with slavery for its corner stone," have become known to the people, — their causeless rebellion; their seizure of the territory and property of the United States; their siege of Washington; their invasion of States which have refused to join them; their bitter, ineradicable, and universal hatred of the people of the free States, and of all who are loyal to the government, have produced a general conviction that slavery (which alone has caused these results, and by which alone the country has been brought to the verge of ruin) must itself be terminated; and that this "privileged class" *must be abolished;* otherwise the unity of the American people must be destroyed, the government overthrown, and constitutional liberty abandoned.

To secure domestic tranquillity is to make it certain by controlling power. It cannot be thus secured while a perpetual uncontrollable cause of civil war exists. The cause, the means, the opportunity of civil war must be removed; the perennial fountain of all our national woes must be destroyed; otherwise "it will be in vain to cry, Peace! peace! There is no peace."

ARE SLAVEHOLDERS ARBITERS OF PEACE AND WAR?

Is the Union so organized that the means of involving the whole country in ruin must be left in the hands of a small privileged class, to be used at their discretion? Must the blessing of peace and good government be dependent upon the sovereign will and pleasure of a handful of treasonable and unprincipled slave-masters?

Has the constitution bound together the peaceable citizen with the insane assassin, so that his murderous knife cannot lawfully be wrenched from his grasp even in self-defence?

If the destruction of slavery be necessary to save the country from defeat, disgrace, and ruin,—and if, at the same time, the constitution guarantees the perpetuity of slavery, whether the country is saved or lost, — it is time that the friends of the government should awake, and realize their awful destiny. If the objects for which our government was founded can lawfully be secured only so far as they do not interfere with the pretensions of slavery, we must admit that the interests of slave-masters stand first, and the welfare of the people of the United States stands last, under the guarantees of the constitution. If the Union, the constitution, and the laws, like Laocoön and his sons, are to be strangled and crushed, in order that the unrelenting serpent may live in triumph, it is time to determine which of them is most worthy to be saved. Such was not the Union formed by our forefathers. Such is not the Union the people intend to preserve. *They* mean to uphold a *Union, under the constitution, interpreted by common sense;* a *government* able to attain results worthy of a great and free people, and for which it was founded; a *republic*, representing the sovereign majesty of the whole nation, clothed with ample powers to maintain its supremacy forever. They mean that liberty and union shall be "one and inseparable."

WHY SLAVERY, THOUGH HATED, WAS TOLERATED.

It is true, that indirectly, and *for the purpose of a more equal distribution of direct taxes,* the framers of the constitution *tolerated*, while they condemned slavery; but they tolerated it because they believed that it would soon disappear. They even refused to allow the charter of their own liberties to be polluted by the mention of the word "slave." Having called the world to witness their heroic and unselfish sacrifices for the vindication of their own inalienable rights, they could not, consistently with honor or self-respect, transmit to future ages the evidence that some of them had trampled upon the inalienable rights of others.

RECOGNITION OF SLAVERY NOT INCONSISTENT WITH THE PERPETUITY OF THE REPUBLIC.

Though slavery was thus tolerated by being ignored, we should dishonor the memory of those who organized that government to suppose that they did not intend to bestow upon it the power to maintain its own authority — the right to overthrow or remove slavery, or whatever might prove fatal to its permanence, or destroy its usefulness. We should discredit the good sense of the great people who ordained and established it, to deny that they bestowed upon the republic, created by and for themselves, the right, the duty, and the powers of *self-defence*. For self-defence by the government was only maintaining, through the people's agents, the right of the people to govern themselves.

DISTINCTION BETWEEN THE OBJECTS AND THE MEANS OF WAR.

We are involved in a war of self-defence.

It is not the *object and purpose* of our hostilities to lay waste lands, burn bridges, break up railroads, sink ships, blockade harbors, destroy commerce, capture, imprison, wound, or kill citizens; to seize, appropriate, confiscate, or destroy private property; to interfere with families, or domestic institutions; to remove, employ, liberate, or arm slaves; to accumulate national debt, impose new and burdensome taxes; or to cause thousands of loyal citizens to be slain in battle. But, as *means of carrying on the contest*, it has become necessary and lawful to lay waste, burn, sink, destroy, blockade, wound, capture, and kill; to accumulate debt, lay taxes, and expose soldiers to the peril of deadly combat. Such are the ordinary results and incidents of war. If, in further prosecuting hostilities, the liberating, employing, or arming of slaves shall be deemed convenient for the more certain, speedy, and effectual overthrow of the enemy, the question will arise, whether the constitution prohibits those measures as acts of legitimate war against rebels, who, having abjured that constitution and having openly in arms defied the government, claim for themselves only the rights of belligerents.

It is fortunate for America that securing the liberties of a great people by giving freedom to four millions of bondmen would be in accordance with the dictates of justice and humanity. If the preservation of the Union required the enslavement of four millions of freemen, very different considerations would be presented.

LIBERAL AND STRICT CONSTRUCTIONISTS.

The friends and defenders of the constitution of the United States of America, ever since its ratification, have expressed widely different opinions regarding the limitation of the powers of government in time of peace, no less than in time of war. Those who have contended for the most narrow and technical construction, having stuck to the letter of the text, and not appreciating the spirit in which it was framed, are opposed to all who view it as only a *frame* of government, a *plan-in-outline*, for regulating the affairs of an enterprising and progressive nation. Some treat that frame of government as though it were a cast-iron mould, incapable of adaptation or alteration — as one which a blow would break in pieces. Others think it a hoop placed around the trunk of a living tree, whose growth must girdle the tree, or burst the hoop. But sounder judges believe that it more resembles the tree itself, — native to the soil that bore it, — waxing strong in sunshine and in storm, putting forth branches, leaves, and roots, according to the laws of its own growth, and flourishing with eternal verdure. Our constitution, like that of England, contains all that is required to adapt itself to the present and future changes and wants of a free and advancing people. This great nation, like a distant planet in the solar system, may sweep round a wide orbit; but in its revolutions it never gets beyond the reach of the central light. The sunshine of constitutional law illumines its pathway in all its changing positions. We have not yet arrived at the "dead point" where the hoop must burst — the mould be shattered — the tree girdled — or the sun shed darkness rather than light. By a liberal construction of the constitution, our government has passed through many storms unharmed. Slaveholding States, other than those whose inhabitants originally formed it, have found their way into the Union, notwithstanding the guarantee of equal rights to all. The territories of Florida and Louisiana have been purchased from European powers. Conquest has added a nation to our borders. The purchased and the conquered regions are now legally a part of the United States. The admission of new States containing a privileged class, the incorporation into our Union of a foreign people, are held to be lawful and valid by all the courts of the country. Thus far from the old anchorage have we sailed under the flag of "public necessity," "general welfare," or "common defence." Yet the great charter of our political rights "still lives;" and the question of to-day is, whether that instrument, which has not prevented America from acquiring one country by purchase, and another by conquest, will permit her to *save herself?*

POWERS WE SHOULD EXPECT TO FIND.

If the ground-plan of our government was intended to be more than a temporary expedient,—if it was designed, according to the declaration of its authors, for a *perpetual* Union,—then it will doubtless be found, upon fair examination, to contain whatever is essential to carry that design into effect. Accordingly, in addition to provisions for adapting it to great changes in the situation and circumstances of the people by *amendments*, we find that powers essential to its own perpetuity are vested in the executive and legislative departments, to be exercised *according to their discretion*, for the good of the country—powers which, however dangerous, must be intrusted to every government, to enable it to maintain its own existence, and to protect the rights of the people. Those who founded a goverment for themselves intended that it should never be overthrown; nor even altered, except by those under whose authority it was established. Therefore they gave to the President, and to Congress, the means essential to the preservation of the republic, but none for its dissolution.

LAWS FOR PEACE, AND LAWS FOR WAR.

Times of peace have required the passage of numerous statutes for the protection and development of agricultural, manufacturing, and commercial industry, and for the suppression and punishment of ordinary crimes and offences. A state of general civil war in the United States is, happily, new and unfamiliar. These times have demanded new and unusual legislation to call into action those powers which the constitution provides for times of war.

Leaving behind us the body of laws regulating the rights, liabilities, and duties of citizens, in time of public tranquillity, we must now turn our attention to the RESERVED and HITHERTO UNUSED powers contained in the constitution, which enable Congress to pass a body of laws to regulate the rights, liabilities, and duties of citizens in time of war. We must enter and explore the arsenal and armory, with all their engines of defence, enclosed, by our wise forefathers for the safety of the republic, within the old castle walls of that constitution; for now the garrison is summoned to surrender; and if there be any cannon, it is time to unlimber and run them out the port-holes, to fetch up the hot shot, to light the match, and hang out our banner on the *outer* walls.

THE UNION IS GONE FOREVER IF THE CONSTITUTION DENIES THE POWER TO SAVE IT.

The question whether republican constitutional government shall now cease in America, must depend upon the construction given to these *hitherto unused powers.* Those who desire to see an end of this government will deny that it has the ability to save itself. Many new inquiries have arisen in relation to the existence and limitation of its powers. Must the successful prosecution of war against rebels, the preservation of national honor, and securing of permanent peace,—if attainable only by rooting out the evil which caused and maintains the rebellion,—be effected by destroying rights solemnly guaranteed by the constitution we are defending? If so, the next question will be, whether the law of self-defence and overwhelming necessity will not justify the country in denying to rebels and traitors in arms whatever rights they or their friends may claim under a charter which they have repudiated, and have armed themselves to overthrow and destroy? Can one party break the contract, and justly hold the other party bound by it? Is the constitution to be so interpreted that rebels and traitors cannot be put down? Are we so hampered, as some have asserted, that even if war end in reëstablishing the Union, and enforcing the laws over all the land, the results of victory will be turned against us, and the conquered enemy may then treat us as though they had been victors? Will vanquished criminals be able to resume their rights to the same political superiority over the citizens of Free States, which, as the only "privileged class," they have hitherto enjoyed?

Have they who alone have made this rebellion, while committing treason and other high crimes against the republic, a protection, an immunity against punishment for these crimes, whether by forfeiture of life or property, by reason of any clause in the constitution? Can government, the people's agent, wage genuine and effectual war against their enemy? or must the soldier of the Union, when in action, keep one eye upon his rifle, and the other upon the constitution? Is the power to make war, when once lawfully brought into action, to be controlled, baffled, and emasculated by any obligation to guard or respect rights set up by or for belligerent traitors?

THE LEADING QUESTIONS STATED.

What limit, if any, is prescribed to the war-making power of the President, as *Commander-in-Chief* of the army and navy of the United States? What authority has Congress to frame laws interfering with the ordinary civil rights of persons and property, of loyal or disloyal citizens, in peaceful or in rebellious districts; of the enemy who may be captured as spies, as pirates, as guerrillas or bush-whackers; as aiders and comforters of armed traitors, or as soldiers in the battle-field? What rights has Congress, or the President, in relation to *belligerent districts* of country; in relation to slaves captured or escaping into the lines of our army, or escaping into Free States; or slaves used by the enemy in military service; or those belonging to rebels, not so used? Whether they are contraband of war? and whether they may be released, manumitted, or emancipated, and discharged by the civil or military authority? or whether slaves may be released from their obligation to serve rebel masters? and whether slavery may be abolished with or without the consent of the masters, as a military measure, or as a legislative act, required by the public welfare and common defence? Where the power to abolish it resides, under the constitution?

And whether there is any restraint or limitation upon the power of Congress to punish treason? What are the rights of government over the private property of loyal citizens? What are the rights and liabilities of traitors? These and similar inquiries are frequently made among the plain people; and it is for the purpose of explaining some of the doctrines of law applicable to them, that the following suggestions have been prepared.

CHAPTER I.

THE CONSTITUTIONAL RIGHT OF THE GOVERNMENT TO APPROPRIATE PRIVATE PROPERTY TO PUBLIC USE, EITHER IN TIME OF PEACE OR IN TIME OF WAR.

The general government of the United States has, in time of peace, a legal right, under the constitution, to appropriate to public use the private property of any subject, or of any number of subjects, owing it allegiance.

Each of the States claims and exercises a similar right over the property of its own citizens.

THE RIGHT IS FOUNDED IN REASON.

All permanent governments in civilized countries assert and carry into effect, in different ways, the claim of "eminent domain;" for it is essential to their authority, and even to their existence. The construction of military defences, such as forts, arsenals, roads, navigable canals, however essential to the protection of a country in war, might be prevented by private interests, if the property of individuals could not be taken by the country, through its government. Internal improvements in time of peace, however important to the interests of the public, requiring the appropriation of real estate belonging to individuals, might be interrupted, if there were no power to *take*, without the consent of the owner, what the public use requires. And as it is the government which protects all citizens in their rights to life, liberty, and property, they are deemed to hold their property subject to the claim of the supreme protector to take it from them when demanded by "public welfare." It is under this quasi *sovereign* power that the State of Massachusetts seizes by law the private estates of her citizens; and she even authorizes several classes of corporations to seize land, against the will of the proprietor, for public use and benefit. Railroads, canals, turnpikes, telegraphs, bridges, aqueducts, could never have been constructed were the existence of this great right denied. And the TITLE to that interest in real estate, which is thus acquired by legal seizure, is deemed by all the courts of this commonwealth to be as legal, and as *constitutional*, as if purchased and conveyed by deed, under the hand and seal of the owner.

INDEMNITY IS REQUIRED.

But, when individuals are called upon to give up what is their own for the advantage of the community, justice requires that they should be fairly compensated for it: otherwise public burdens would be shared unequally. To secure the right to indemnification, which was omitted in the original constitution of the United States, an amendment was added, which provides, (Amendments, Art. V, last clause,) "*Nor shall private property be taken for public use without just compensation.*" *

The language of this *amendment* admits the right of the United States to take private property for public use. This amendment, being now a part of the constitution, leaves that right no longer open to question, if it ever was questioned.

* Similar provisions are found in the constitution of Massachusetts, and several other states.

In guarding against the abuse of the right to take private property for public use, it is provided that the owner shall be entitled to be fairly paid for it; and thus he is not to be taxed *more than his due share* for public purposes.

It is not a little singular that the framers of the constitution should have been *less* careful to secure equality in distributing the burden of taxes. Sect. 8 requires *duties, imposts, and excises* to be *uniform* throughout the United States, but it does not provide that *taxes* should be uniform. Although Art. I., Sect. 9, provides that no *capitation* or other *direct tax* shall be laid unless in proportion to the census, yet far the most important subjects of taxation are still unprotected, and may be UNEQUALLY assessed, without violating any clause of that constitution, which so carefully secures equality of public burdens by providing compensation for private property appropriated to the public benefit.

"PUBLIC USE."

What is "*public use*" for which private property may be taken?

Every appropriation of property for *the benefit* of the United States, either for a national public improvement, or to carry into effect any valid law of Congress for the maintenance, protection, or security of national interests, is "public *use*." *Public use* is contradistinguished from *private use*. That which is for the *use of the country*, however applied or appropriated, is for public use.

Public use does not require that the property taken shall be actually *used*. It may be *disused, removed*, or *destroyed*. And destruction of private property may be the best public use it can be put to.

Suppose a bridge, owned by a private corporation, were so located as to endanger a military work upon the bank of a river. The *destruction* of that bridge to gain a military advantage would be appropriating it to *public use.*

So also the blowing up or demolition of buildings in a city, for the purpose of preventing a general conflagration, would be an appropriation of them to public use. The *destruction* of arms, or other munitions of war, belonging to private persons, in order to prevent their falling into possession of the enemy, would be applying them to *public use.* Congress has power to pass laws providing for the common defence and general welfare, under Art. I. Sect. 8 of the constitution; and whenever, in their judgment, the common defence or general welfare requires them to authorize the appropriation of private property to public use, — whether that use be *the employment or destruction of the property taken,* — they have the right to pass such laws; to appropriate private property in that way; and whatever is done with it is "public use," and entitles the owner to just compensation therefor.

ALL KINDS OF PROPERTY, INCLUDING SLAVES, MAY BE SO APPROPRIATED.

There is no restriction as to the kind or *character* of private property which may be lawfully thus appropriated, whether it be real estate, personal estate, rights in action or in possession, *obligations for money, or for labor and service.* Thus the obligations of minor children to their parents, of apprentices to their masters, and of other persons owing labor and service to their masters, may lawfully be appropriated to public use, or discharged and destroyed, for public benefit, by Congress, with the proviso that just compensation shall be allowed to the parent or master.

Our government, by treaty, discharged the claims of its own citizens against France, and thus appropriated private property to public use. At a later date the United States discharged the claims of certain slave owners to labor and service, whose slaves had been carried away by the British contrary to their treaty stipulations. In both cases indemnity was promised by our government to the owners; and in case of the slave masters it was actually paid. By abolishing slavery in the District of Columbia, that which was considered for the purposes of the act as private property was appropriated to public use, with just compensation to the owners; Congress, in this instance, having the right to pass the act as a local, municipal law; but the compensation was from the treasury of the United States.

During the present rebellion, many minors, apprentices, and slaves have been relieved from obligation to their parents and masters, the claim for their services having been appropriated to public use, by employing them in the military service of the country.

That Congress should have *power* to appropriate *every description* of private property for public benefit in time of war, results from the *duty* imposed on it by the constitution to pass laws "providing for the common defence and general welfare."

Suppose that a large number of apprentices desired to join the army as volunteers in time of sorest need, but were restrained from so doing only by reason of their owing labor and service to their employers, who were equally with them citizens and subjects of this government; would any one doubt or deny the right of government to accept these apprentices as soldiers, to discharge them from the obligation of their indentures, providing just compensation to their employers for loss of their services? Suppose that these volunteers owed labor and service for life, as slaves, instead of owing it for a term of years; what difference could it make as to the right of government to use their services, and discharge their obligations, or as to the liability to indemnify the masters? The right to use the services of the minor, the apprentice, and the slave, for public benefit, belongs to the United States. The claims of all American citizens upon their services, whether by local law, or by common law, or by indentures, can be annulled by the same power, for the same reasons, and under the same restrictions that govern the appropriation of any other private property to public use.

THE UNITED STATES MAY REQUIRE ALL SUBJECTS TO DO MILITARY DUTY.

Slaves, as well as apprentices and minors, are equally *subjects* of the United States, whether they are or are not *citizens* thereof. The government of the United States has the right to call upon all its subjects to do *military duty*. If those who owe labor and service to others, either by contract, by indenture, by common or statute law, or by local usage, could not be lawfully called upon to *leave* their employments to serve their country, no inconsiderable portion of the able-bodied men would thus be ex empt, and the constitution and laws of the land providing for calling out the army and navy would be set at nought. But the constitution makes no such exemptions from military duty. Private rights cannot be set up to overthrow the claims of the country to the services of every one of its subjects who owes it allegiance.

How far the United States is under obligation to compensate parents, masters of apprentices, or masters of slaves, for the loss of service and labor of those subjects who are enlisted in the army and navy, has not been yet decided.* The constitution recognizes slaves as "*persons held to labor or service.*" So also are apprentices and minor children "persons held to labor and service." And, whatever other claims may be set up, by the laws of either of the slave states, to any class of "persons," the constitution recognizes *only* the claim of individuals to *the labor and service* of other individuals. It seems difficult, therefore, to state any sound principle which should require compensation in one case and not in the other.

WILL SLAVEHOLDERS BE ENTITLED TO INDEMNITY IF THEIR SLAVES ARE USED FOR MILITARY PURPOSES?

It is by no means improbable, that, in the emergency which we are fast approaching, the right and duty of the country to call upon *all* its *loyal subjects* to aid in its military defence *will be deemed paramount to the claims of any private person upon such subjects*, and that the

* If an apprentice enlist in the army, the courts will not, upon a *habeas corpus*, issued at the relation of the master, *remand* the apprentice to his custody, if he be *unwilling* to return, but will leave the master to his suit against the officer, who, by Stat. 16 Mar. 1802, was forbidden to enlist him without the master's consent. *Commonwealth* v. *Robinson*, 1 S. & R. 353; *Commonwealth* v. *Harris*, 7 Pa. L. J. 283.

loss of *labor and service* of certain citizens, like the loss of life and property, which always attends a state of war, must be borne by those upon whom the misfortune happens to fall. It may become one of the great political questions hereafter, whether, if slavery should as a civil act in time of peace, or by treaty in time of war, be wholly or partly abolished, for *public benefit*, or *public defence*, such abolishment is *an appropriation* of *private property* for public use, *within the meaning of the constitution.*

INDEMNITY TO MORMONS.

The question has not yet arisen in the courts of the United States, whether the act of Congress, which, under the form of a statute against polygamy abolishes Mormonism, a domestic institution, sustained like slavery only by local law, is such an appropriation of the claims of Mormons to the labor and service of their wives as requires just compensation under the constitution? A decision of this question may throw some light on the point now under consideration.

EFFECT OF NATURALIZATION AND MILITIA LAWS ON THE QUESTION OF INDEMNITY TO SLAVE-MASTERS.

A further question may arise as to the application of the "compensation" clause above referred to. Congress has the power to pass naturalization laws, by Art. I. Sect. 8. This power has never been doubted. The only question is, whether this power is not exclusive.* Congress may thus give the privileges of citizenship to

* See *Chirac* v. *Chirac,* 2 Whea. 269; *U. S.* v. *Villato,* 2 Dall. 372; *Thirlow* v. *Mass.,* 5 How. 585; *Smith* v. *Turner,* 7 ib. 556; *Golden* v. *Prince,* 3 W. C. C. P., 314.

any persons whatsoever, black or white. Colored men, having been citizens in *some* of the *States* ever since they were founded, having acted as citizens prior to 1788 in various civil and military capacities, are therefore citizens of the United States.*

Under the present laws of the United States, according to the opinion of the attorney-general of Massachusetts, *colored men are equally with white men required to be enrolled in the militia of the United States*,† although such was not the case under the previous acts of 1792 and 1795. "The general government has authority to determine who shall and who may not compose the militia of the United States; and having so determined, the state government has no legal authority to prescribe a different enrolment.‡ If, therefore, Congress exercise either of these undoubted powers to grant *citizenship* to all colored persons residing or coming within either of the States, or to pass an act requiring *the enrolment* of all able-bodied persons within a prescribed age, whether owing labor and service or not, as *part of the militia of the United States*, and thereby giving to all, as they become soldiers or seamen, their freedom from obligations of labor and service, except *military* labor and service, then the question would arise, whether government, by calling its own subjects and citizens into the military service of the country, in case of overwhelming necessity, could be required by the constitution to recognize the private relations in which the soldier might stand, by *local* laws, to persons setting up

* See case of *Dred Scott;* which in no part denies that if colored men *were* citizens of either of the states which adopted the constitution, they were citizens of the United States.

† See Stat. U. S. July 17, 1862.

‡ 8 Gray's R. 615.

claims against him? If white subjects or citizens, owe labor and service, even by formal indentures, such obligations afford no valid excuse against the requisition of government to have them drafted into the militia to serve the country. The government does not compensate those who claim indemnity for the loss of such "labor and service." Whether the *color* of the debtor, or the *length* of time during which the obligation (to labor and service) has to run, or the *evidence* by which the *existence* of the obligation is proved, can make an essential difference between the different kinds of labor and service, remains to be seen. The question is, whether the soldier or seaman, serving his country in arms, can be deemed *private property*, as recognized in the constitution of the United States?

DOES THE WAR POWER OF SEIZURE SUPERSEDE THE CIVIL POWER OF CONGRESS TO APPROPRIATE PRIVATE PROPERTY TO PUBLIC USE?

That the property of any citizen may, under certain circumstances, be seized in time of war, by *military officers*, for public purposes, is not questioned, just compensation being offered, or provided for; but the question has been asked, whether this power does not supersede the right of Congress, in war, to pass laws to take away what martial law leaves unappropriated?

This inquiry is conclusively answered by reference to the amendment of the constitution, above cited, which admits the existence of that power in CONGRESS;* but in addition to this, there are other clauses which devolve powers and duties on the legislature, giving them a large and important share in instituting, organizing, carrying on, regulating, and ending war; and these duties could not, under all circumstances, be discharged

* Amendments, Art. V. last clause.

in war, without exercising the right to take for public use the property of the subject. It would seem strange if private property could not be so taken, while it is undeniable that in war the government can call into the military service of the country every able-bodied citizen, and tax his property to any extent.

REFERENCES AS TO THE CONSTITUTION, SHOWING THE WAR POWERS OF CONGRESS.

The powers of the *legislative* department in relation to war are contained chiefly in the following sections in the constitution: —

Art. I., Sect. 8, Cl. 11. *Congress* may *institute* war by declaring it against an enemy. The President alone cannot do so. Also, Congress may make laws concerning *captures on land*, as well as *on water*.

Art. I., Sect. 8, Cl. 12. Congress may *raise and support armies:* and provide and maintain a navy.

Art. I., Sect. 8, Cl. 14. Congress may make laws for the *government* of land and naval forces.

Art. I., Sect. 8, Cl. 15. Congress may provide for *calling forth* the militia to execute the laws of the Union, suppress insurrection, and repel invasion.

Art. I., Sect. 8, Cl. 16: And may provide for organizing, arming, and disciplining the militia, and for *governing* such part of them as may be employed in the service of the United States.

The preamble to the constitution declares the objects for which it was framed to be these: "to form a more perfect Union; establish justice; *insure domestic tranquillity;* provide for *the common defence;* promote the general welfare, and secure the blessings of liberty to ourselves and our posterity." In Art. I., Sect. 8, Cl. 1, the *first power* given to Congress is to lay and collect taxes, duties, imposts, and excises, to pay the debts, and provide for the *common defence and general welfare of the United States.* And in the same article (the eighteenth clause) express power is given to Congress *to make all laws which shall be necessary and proper for carrying into execution the foregoing and all other powers vested by the constitution in the government of the United States, or in any department or officer thereof.*"

SLAVE PROPERTY SUBJECT TO THE SAME LIABILITY AS OTHER PROPERTY TO BE APPROPRIATED FOR WAR PURPOSES.

If the *public welfare*, or *common defence*, in time of war, requires that the claims of masters over their apprentices or slaves should be cancelled or abrogated, against their consent, and if a general law carrying into execution such abrogation, is, in the judgment of Congress, "a necessary and proper measure for accomplishing that object," there can be no question of the constitutional power and right of Congress to pass such laws. The only doubt is in relation to the right to compensation. If it should be said that the release of slaves from their servitude would be tantamount to impairing or destroying the obligation of contracts, it may be said, that though states have no right to pass laws impairing the obligation of contracts, Congress is at liberty to pass such laws. It will be readily perceived that the right to abrogate and cancel the obligations of apprentices and slaves does not rest solely upon the power of Congress to appropriate private property to public use; but it may be founded upon their power and obligation to accomplish one of the chief objects for which the Union was formed, viz., to provide for the *common defence* and *general welfare* of the United States.

IMPORTANCE AND DANGER OF THIS POWER.

The powers conveyed in this 18th clause of Art. I., Sect. 8, are of *vast* importance and extent. It may be said that they are, in one sense, unlimited and discretionary. They are more than imperial. But it was intended by the framers of the constitution, or, what is of more importance, by the *people* who made and adopted it, that the powers of government in dealing with civil rights in time of peace, should be *defined* and limited; but the powers "to provide for the *general welfare* and the *common défence*" should be *unlimited.* It is true that such powers may be temporarily abused; but the remedy is always in the hands of the people, who can unmake laws and select new representatives and senators.

POWERS OF THE PRESIDENT NOT IN CONFLICT WITH THOSE OF CONGRESS.

It is not necessary here to define the extent to which congressional legislation may justly control and regulate the conduct of the army and navy in service; or where falls the dividing line between civil and martial law. But the power of Congress to pass laws on the subjects expressly placed in its charge by the terms of the constitution cannot be taken away from it, by reason of the fact that the President, as commander-in-chief of the army and navy, also has powers, equally constitutional, to act upon the same subject-matters. It does not follow that because Congress has power to abrogate the claims of Mormons or slaveholders, the President, as commander, may not also do the same thing.

These powers are not *inconsistent*, or conflicting. Congress may pass laws concerning *captures* on land

and on the water. If slaves are *captured,* and are treated as "captured property," Congress should determine what is to be done with them;* and it will be the President's duty to see that *these* as well as other laws of the United States are *executed.*

CONGRESS HAS POWER UNDER THE CONSTITUTION TO ABOLISH SLAVERY.

Whenever, in the judgment of Congress, the common defence and public welfare require the removal of the condition of slavery, it is within the scope of their constitutional authority to pass laws for that purpose.

If such laws are deemed to take private property for public use, or to destroy private property for public benefit, as has been shown, that may be done under the constitution, by providing just compensation; otherwise, no compensation can be required. It has been so long the habit of those who engage in public life to disclaim any intention to interfere with slavery in the States, that they have of late become accustomed to deny the *right of Congress* to do so. But *the constitution contains no clause or sentence prohibiting the exercise by Congress of the plenary power of abrogating involuntary servitude.* The only prohibition contained in that instrument relating to persons held to labor and service, is in Art. IV., which provides that, "No person held to labor and service in one state, *under the laws thereof,* escaping into another, shall, in consequence of any *law* or *regulation* "*therein,*" be discharged from such service or labor; but shall be delivered up on claim of the party to whom such service or labor may be due." Thus, if a slave or appren-

* Constitution, Art. I., Sect. 8, Cl. 11.

tice, owing service to his employer in Maryland, escapes to New York, the legislature of New York cannot, by any law or regulation, legally discharge such apprentice or slave from his liability to his employer. *This restriction is, in express terms, applicable only to State legislatures, and not to Congress.*

Many powers given to Congress are denied to the States; and there are obvious reasons why the supreme government alone should exercise so important a right. That a power is withdrawn from the States, indicates, by fair implication, that *it belongs to the United States,* unless expressly prohibited, if it is embraced within the scope of powers necessary to the safety and preservation of the government, in peace or in civil war.

It will be remarked that the provision as to slaves in the constitution relates only to fugitives from labor escaping from one state into another; not to the *status* or *condition* of slaves in any of the states where they are held, while another clause in the constitution relates to *fugitives* from justice.* Neither clause has any application to citizens or persons who are not *fugitives.* And it would be a singular species of reasoning to conclude that, because the constitution prescribed certain rules of conduct towards persons *escaping from one State into another,* therefore there is no power to make rules relating *to other persons who do not escape from one State into another.* If Congress were expressly empowered to pass laws relating to persons *when escaping* from justice or labor by fleeing from their own States, it would be absurd to infer that there could be no power to pass laws relating to these same persons when staying at home. The govern-

* Constitution, Art. IV. Sect. 2.

ment may pass laws requiring the return of fugitives: they may pass other laws punishing their crimes, or relieving them from penalty. The power to do the one by no means negatives the power to do the other. If Congress should discharge the obligations of slaves to render labor and service, by passing a law to that effect, such law would supersede and render void all rules, regulations, customs, or laws of either State to the contrary, for the constitution, treaties, and laws of the United States are the supreme law of the land. If slaves were released by act of Congress, or by the act of their masters, there would be no person *held to labor* as a slave by the laws of *any State,* and therefore there would be no person to whom the clause in the constitution restraining State legislation could apply. This clause, relating to fugitive slaves, has often been misunderstood, as it has been supposed to limit the power of *Congress,* while in fact *it applies in plain and express terms only to the States,* controlling or limiting *their* powers, but having no application to the general government. If the framers of the constitution intended to take from Congress the power of passing laws relating to slaves in the States or elsewhere, they would have drafted a clause to that effect. They did insert in that instrument a proviso that Congress should pass no law prohibiting the "importation of such persons as any of the States should think proper to admit" (meaning slaves) "prior to 1808." * And if they did not design that the legislature should exercise control over the subject of domestic slavery, whenever it should assume such an aspect as to involve *national* interests, the introduction of the proviso relating to the slave

* Constitution, Art. I. Sect. 9.

trade, and of several other clauses in the plan of government, makes the omission of any prohibition of legislation on slavery unaccountable.

CONCLUSION.

Thus it has been shown that the government have the right to appropriate to public use *private property* of every description; that "public use" may require the employment or the destruction of such property; that if the "right to the labor and service of others," as slaves, be recognized in the broadest sense as "property," there is nothing in the constitution which deprives Congress of the power to appropriate "that description of property" to public use, by terminating slavery, whenever laws to that effect are required by "public welfare and common defence;" that this power is left to the discretion of Congress, who are the sole and exclusive judges as to the occasions when it shall be exercised, and from whose judgment there is no appeal. The right to "just compensation" for private property so taken, depends upon the circumstances under which it is taken, and the loyalty and other legal conditions of the claimant.

NOTE.—As to the use of discretionary powers in *other* departments, see *Martin* v. *Mott*, 12 Wheat. 29–31; *Luther* v. *Borden*, 7 How. 44, 45.

5

CHAPTER II.

WAR POWERS OF CONGRESS.*

CONGRESS has power to frame statutes not only for the punishment of crimes, but also for the purpose of aiding the President, as commander-in-chief of the army and navy, in suppressing rebellion, and in the final and permanent conquest of a public enemy. "It may pass such laws as it may deem necessary," says Chief Justice Marshall, "to carry into execution the great powers granted by the constitution;" and "necessary means, in the sense of the constitution, does not import an absolute physical necessity, so strong that one thing cannot exist without the other. It stands for any means calculated to produce the end."

RULES OF INTERPRETATION.

The constitution provides that Congress shall have power to pass "all laws necessary and proper" for carrying into execution all the powers granted to the government of the United States, or any department or officer thereof. The word "necessary," as used, is not limited by the additional word "proper," but enlarged thereby.

"If the word *necessary* were used in the strict, rigorous sense, it would be an extraordinary departure from the usual course of the human mind, as exhibited in solemn instruments, to add another word, the only possible effect of which is to qualify that strict and rigorous meaning, and to present clearly the idea of a choice of means in the course of legislation. If no means are to be resorted to but such as

* For references to the clauses of the Constitution containing the war powers of Congress, see *ante*, pp. 27, 28.

are *indispensably* necessary, there can be neither sense nor utility in adding the word '*proper*,' for the *indispensable necessity* would shut out from view all consideration of the *propriety* of the means." *

Alexander Hamilton says,—

"The authorities essential to the care of the common defence are these: To raise armies; to build and equip fleets; to prescribe rules for the government of both; to direct their operations; to provide for their support. These powers ought to exist WITHOUT LIMITATION, because it is impossible to foresee or to define the extent and variety of national exigencies, and the correspondent extent and variety of the means necessary to satisfy them. The circumstances which endanger the safety of nations are infinite; and for this reason no constitutional shackles can wisely be imposed on the power to which the care of it is committed. . . . This power ought to be under the direction of the same councils which are appointed to preside over the *common defence*. . . . It must be admitted, as a necessary consequence, that there can be no limitation of that authority which is to provide for the defence and protection of the community in any matter essential to its efficacy—that is, in any matter essential to the *formation*, *direction*, or *support* of the NATIONAL FORCES."

This statement, Hamilton says,—

"Rests upon two axioms, simple as they are universal: the *means* ought to be proportioned to the *end;* the persons from whose agency the attainment of the *end* is expected, ought to possess the *means* by which it is to be attained." †

The doctrine of the Supreme Court of the United States, announced by Chief Justice Marshall, and approved by Daniel Webster, Chancellor Kent, and Judge Story, is thus stated:—

"The government of the United States is one of enumerated powers, and it can exercise only the powers granted to it; but though limited in its powers, it is supreme within its sphere of action. It is the government of the people of the United States, and emanated from them. Its powers were delegated by all, and it represents all, and acts for all.

"There is nothing in the constitution which excludes *incidental* or

* 3 Story's Commentaries, Sec. 122. † Federalist, No. 23, pp. 95, 96.

implied powers. The Articles of Confederation gave nothing to the United States but what was expressly granted; but the new constitution dropped the word *expressly*, and left the question whether a particular power was granted to depend on a fair construction of the whole instrument. No constitution can contain an accurate detail of all the subdivisions of its powers, and all the *means* by which they might be carried into execution. It would render it too prolix. Its nature requires that only the great outlines should be marked, and its important objects designated, and all the minor ingredients left to be deduced from the nature of those objects. The sword and the purse, all the external relations, and no inconsiderable portion of the industry of the nation, were intrusted to the general government; and a government intrusted with such ample powers, on the due execution of which the happiness and prosperity of the people vitally depended, must also be intrusted with *ample means of their execution.* Unless the words imperiously require it, we ought not to adopt a construction which would impute to the framers of the constitution, when granting great powers for the public good, the intention of impeding their exercise by withholding a *choice of means.* The powers given to the government imply the ordinary means of execution; and the government, in all sound reason and fair interpretation, must have the choice of the means which it deems the most convenient and appropriate to the execution of the power. The constitution has not left the right of Congress to employ the necesssary means for the execution of its powers to general reasoning. Art. I, Sect. 8, of the constitution, expressly confers on Congress the power 'to make all laws that may be necessary and proper to carry into execution the foregoing powers.'

"Congress may employ such means and pass such laws as it may deem necessary to carry into execution great powers granted by the constitution; and *necessary* means, in the sense of the constitution, does not import an absolute physical necessity, so strong that one thing cannot exist without the other. It stands for any means calculated to produce the end. The word *necessary* admits of all degress of comparison. A thing may be necessary, or very necessary, or absolutely or indispensably necessary. The word is used in various senses, and in its construction the subject, the context, the intention, are all to be taken into view. The powers of the government were given for the welfare of the nation. They were intended to endure for ages to come, and to be adapted to the various *crises* in human affairs. To prescribe the specific means by which government should in all future time execute its power, and to confine the choice of means to such narrow limits as should not leave it in the power of Congress to adopt any which might be appropriate and conducive to the end, would be most unwise and pernicious, because it would be an attempt to provide, by immutable rules, for exigencies which, if foreseen at all, must have been foreseen dimly, and would deprive the legislature of the capacity to avail itself of experience, or to exercise its reason, and accommodate its legislation to circumstances. If the end be legitimate, and within the scope of the constitution, all means which are appropriate, and plainly adapted to this end, and which are not prohibited by the constitution, are lawful." *

Guided by these principles of interpretation, it is obvious that if the confiscation of property, or the liberation of slaves of rebels, be "plainly adapted to the end," — that is, to the suppression of rebellion, — it is within the power of Congress to pass laws for those purposes. Whether they are adapted to produce that result is for the legislature alone to decide. But, in considering the war powers conferred upon that department of government, a broad distinction is to be observed between confiscation or emancipation laws, passed in time of peace, for the punishment of crime, and similar laws, passed in time of war, to aid the President in suppressing rebellion, in carrying on a civil war, and in securing "the public welfare" and maintaining the "common defence" of the country. Congress may pass such laws in peace or in war as are within the general powers conferred on it, unless they fall within some express prohibition of the constitution. If confiscation or emancipation laws are enacted under the war powers of Congress, we must determine, in order to test their validity, whether, in suppressing a rebellion of colossal proportions, the United States are, within the meaning of

* On the interpretation of constitutional power, see 1 Kent's Com. 351, 352; *McCulloch* v. *The State of Maryland*, 4 Wheat. R. 413–420.

the constitution, *at war* with its own citizens? whether confiscation and emancipation are sanctioned as belligerent rights by the law and usage of civilized nations? and whether our government has full belligerent rights against its rebellious subjects?

ARE THE UNITED STATES AT WAR?

War may originate in either of several ways. The navy of a European nation may attack an American frigate in a remote sea. Hostilities then commence without any invasion of the soil of America, or any insurrection of its inhabitants. A foreign power may send troops into our territory with hostile intent, and without declaration of war; yet war would exist solely by this act of invasion. Congress, on one occasion, passed a resolution that "war existed by the act of Mexico;" but no declaration of war had been made by either belligerent. Civil war may commence either as a general armed insurrection of slaves, a servile war; or as an insurrection of their masters, a rebellion; or as an attempt, by a considerable portion of the subjects, to overthrow their government—which attempt, if successful, is termed a revolution. Civil war, within the meaning of the constitution, exists also whenever any combination of citizens is formed to resist generally the execution of any one or of all the laws of the United States, if accompanied with overt acts to give that resistance effect.

DECLARATION OF WAR NOT NECESSARY ON THE PART OF THE GOVERNMENT TO GIVE IT FULL BELLIGERENT POWERS.

A state of war may exist, arising in either of the modes above mentioned, without a declaration of war by either of the hostile parties. Congress has the sole power, under the constitution, to make that declaration, and to sanction or authorize the commencement of *offensive* war. If the United States commence hostilities against a foreign nation, such commencement is by proclamation, which is equivalent to a declaration of war. But this is quite a different case from a defensive or a civil war. The constitution establishes the mode in which this government shall *commence* wars, and what authority shall ordain, and what declarations shall precede, any act of hostility; but it has no power to prescribe the manner in which others should begin war against us. Hence it follows, that when war is commenced against this country, by aliens or by citizens, no declaration of war by the government is necessary. The fact that war is levied against the United States, makes it the duty of the President to call out the army or navy to subdue the enemy, whether foreign or domestic. The chief object of a declaration of war is to give notice thereof to neutrals, in order to fix their rights, and liabilities to the hostile powers, and to give to innocent parties reasonable time to withdraw their persons and property from danger. If the commander-in-chief could not call out his forces to repel an invasion until Congress should have made a formal declaration of war, a foreign army might march from Canada to the Gulf before such declaration could be made, if it should commence the campaign while Congress was not in session. Before a majority of its members could be convened, our navy might be swept from the seas. The constitution, made as it was by men of sense, never leaves the nation powerless for self-defence. That instrument, which gives the legislature authority to declare war, whenever war is *initiated* by the United States, also makes it the duty of the President, as commander-in-chief, to engage promptly and effectually in war; or, in other words, to make the United States a belligerent nation, without declaration of war, or any other act of Congress, whenever he is legally called upon to suppress rebellion, repel invasion, or to execute the laws against armed and forcible resistance thereto. The President has his duty, Congress have theirs; they are separate, and in some respects independent. Nothing is clearer than this, that when such a state of hostilities exists as justifies the President in calling the army into actual service, without the authority of Congress, no declaration of war is requisite, either in form or substance, for any purpose whatsoever. Hence it follows, that government, while engaged in suppressing a rebellion, is not deprived of the rights of a *belligerent against rebels,* by reason of the fact that no formal declaration of war has been made against them, as though they were an alien enemy, — nor by reason of the circumstance that this great civil war originated, so far as we are parties to it, in an effort to resist an armed attack of citizens upon the soldiers and the forts of the United States. It must not be forgotten that by the law of nations and by modern usage, no formal *declaration* of war *to the enemy* is made or deemed necessary.* All that is now requisite is for each nation to make suitable declarations or proclamations to its own citizens, to enable them to govern themselves accordingly. These have been made by the President.

HAS GOVERNMENT FULL WAR POWERS AGAINST REBEL CITIZENS?

Some persons have questioned the right of the United States to make and carry on war against citi-

* See 1 Kent's Com. p. 54.

zens and subjects of this country. Conceding that the President may be authorized to call into active service the navy and army "to repel invasion, or suppress rebellion," they neither admit that suppressing rebellion places the country in the attitude of making war on rebels, nor that the commander-in-chief has the constitutional right of conducting his military operations as he might do if he were actually at war (in the ordinary sense of the term) against an alien enemy. Misapprehension of the meaning of the constitution on this subject has led to confusion in the views of some members of Congress during the last session, and has in no small degree emasculated the efforts of the majority in dealing with the questions of emancipation, confiscation, and enemy's property.

Some have assumed that the United States are not *at war* with rebels, and that they have no authority to exercise the rights of war against them. They admit that the army has been lawfully called into the field, and may kill those who oppose them; they concede that rebels may be taken captive, their gunboats may be sunk, and their property may be seized; that martial law may be declared in rebellious districts, and its pains and penalties may be enforced; that every armed foe may be swept out of the country by military power. Yet they entertain a vague apprehension that something in the constitution takes away from these military proceedings, in suppressing rebellion and in resisting the attacks of the rebels, the quality and character of warfare. All these men in arms are not, they fancy, "*making war*." When the citizens of Charleston bombarded Fort Sumter, and captured property exclusively owned by the United States, it is not

6

denied that *they* were "*waging war*" upon the government. When Major Anderson returned the enemy's fire and attempted to defend the fort and the guns from capture, it is *denied* that the *country* was "waging war." While other nations, as well as our own, had formally or informally conceded to the rebels the character and the rights usually allowed to belligerents, — that is, to persons making war *on us*, — *we*, according to the constitutional scruple above stated, were not entitled to the rights of belligerents against them. It therefore becomes important to know what, according to the constitution, the meaning of the term "levying war" really is; and as the military forces of this country are in actual service to suppress rebellion, whether such military service is *making war* upon its own citizens; and if war actually exists, whether there is any thing in the constitution that limits or controls the full enjoyment and exercise by the government of the rights of a belligerent against the belligerent enemy?

IS "SUPPRESSING REBELLION" BY ARMS MAKING WAR ON THE CITIZENS OF THE UNITED STATES, IN THE SENSE OF THE CONSTITUTION?

To "repel invasion" by arms, all admit, is entering upon defensive war against the invader. War exists wherever and whenever the army or navy is in active service against a public enemy.

When *rebels* are organized into armies in large numbers, overthrow the government, invade the territory of States not consenting thereto, attack, and seize, and confiscate the property not of the government only, but of all persons who continue loyal, such proceedings constitute war in all its terrors — a war of subjugation and of conquest, as well as of rebellion. Far *less* than these operations constitutes the *levying of war*, as those terms are explained in the language of the constitution.

"*War is levied*" on the United States wherever and whenever the crime of *treason* is committed, (see Constitution, Art. III., Sect. 3, Cl. 3,) and under that clause, as interpreted by the Supreme Court, "*war is levied*" when there exists a combination resorting to overt acts to oppose generally the execution of any law of the United States, even if no *armed* force be used. The language of the constitution is clear and express. "Treason shall consist only in levying war upon the United States, or in giving aid and comfort to the enemy." If, therefore, any person, or collection of persons, have committed the crime of treason, the constitution declares them to have *levied war*. As *traitors* they have become belligerent, or war levying enemies.

War may be waged *against* the government or *by* the government; it may be either offensive or defensive. Wherever war exists there must be two parties to it. If traitors (belligerents by the terms of the constitution) are one party, the government is the other party. If, when treason is committed, any body is at war, then it follows that the United States are at war. The inhabitants of a section of this country have issued a manifesto claiming independence; they have engaged in open war on land and sea to maintain it; they have invaded territory of peaceful and loyal sections of the Union; they have seized and confiscated ships, arsenals, arms, forts, public and private property of our government and people, and have killed, captured, and imprisoned soldiers and private citizens. Of the million of men in arms, are those on one side levying war, and are those opposed to them *not* levying war?

As it takes two parties to carry on war, either party may begin it. That party which begins usually declares war. But when it is actually begun, the party attacked is as much at war as the party who made the attack. The United States are AT WAR with rebels, in the strictly legal and constitutional sense of the term, and have therefore all the rights against them which follow from a state of *war*, in addition to those which are derived from the fact that the rebels are also subjects.

REBELS MAY BE TREATED AS BELLIGERENTS AND AS SUBJECTS.

Wars may be divided into two classes, foreign and civil. In all civil wars the government claims the belligerents, on both sides, as subjects, and has the legal right to treat the insurgents both as subjects and as belligerents; and they therefore may exercise the full and untrammelled powers of war against their subjects, or they may, in their discretion, relieve them from any of the pains and penalties attached to either of these characters. The right of a country to treat its rebellious citizens *both as belligerents and as subjects* has long been recognized in Europe, and by the Supreme Court of the United States. In the civil war between St. Domingo and France, such rights were exercised, and were recognized as legitimate in *Rose* v. *Himely*, 4 Cranch, 272. So in *Cherriot* v. *Foussatt*, 3 Binney, 252. In *Dobrie* v. *Napier*, 3 Scott R. 225, it was held that a blockade of the coast of Portugal, by the Queen of that country, was lawful, and a vessel was condemned as a *lawful prize* for running the blockade. The cases of the *Santisima Trinidad*, 7 Wheat. 306, and *United States* v. *Palmer*, 3 W. 635, confirm this doctrine. By the terms of the constitution defining treason, a traitor *must be a subject and a belligerent*, and none but a belligerent subject can be a traitor.

The government have in fact treated the insurgents *as belligerents* on several occasions, without recognizing them in express terms as such. They have received the capitulation of rebels at Hatteras, as prisoners of war, *in express terms*, and have exchanged prisoners of war as such, and have blockaded the coast by military authority, and have officially informed other nations of such blockade, and of their intention to make it effective, under the present law of nations. They have not exercised their undoubted right to repeal the laws making either of the blockaded harbors ports of entry. They have relied solely on their *belligerent* rights, under the law of nations.

Having thus the full powers and right of making and carrying on war against rebels, both as subjects and as belligerents, this *right* frees the President and Congress from the difficulties which might arise if rebels could be treated *only* as SUBJECTS, and if *war* could not be waged upon them. If conceding to rebels the privileges of belligerents should relieve them from some of the harsher penalties of treason, it will subject them to the liabilities of the belligerent character. The privileges and the disadvantages are correlative. But it is by no means conceded that the government may not exercise the right of treating the same rebels both as subjects and as belligerents. The constitution defines a rebel who commits treason as one who "levies war" on the United States; and the laws punish this highest of crimes with death, thus expressly treating the same person *as subject and as belligerent.* Those who save their necks from the halter by claiming to be treated as prisoners of war, and so to protect themselves under the shield of belligerent rights, must bear the weight of that shield, and submit to the legal consequences of the character they claim. They cannot sail under two flags at the same time. But a rebel does not cease to be a subject because he has turned traitor. The constitution expressly authorizes Congress to pass laws to punish traitor—that is, belligerent—subjects; and suppressing rebellion by armed force is making war. Therefore the war powers of government give full belligerent rights against rebels in arms.

THE LAW OF NATIONS IS ABOVE THE CONSTITUTION.

Having shown that the United States being actually engaged in civil war,—in other words, having become a belligerent power, without formal declaration of war,—it is important to ascertain what some of the *rights* of *belligerents* are, according to the law of nations. It will be observed that the law of nations is above the constitution of any government; and no people would be justified by its peculiar constitution in violating the rights of other nations. Thus, if it had been provided in the Articles of Confederation, or in the present constitution, that all citizens should have the inalienable right to practise the profession of *piracy* upon the ships and property of foreign nations, or that they should be lawfully empowered to make incursions into England, France, or other countries, and seize by force and bring home such men and women as they should select, and, if these privileges should be put in practice, England

and France would be justified in treating us as a nest of pirates, or a band of marauders and outlaws. The whole civilized world would turn against us, and we should justly be exterminated. An association or agreement on our part to violate the rights of others, by whatever name it may be designated, whether it be called a constitution, or league, or conspiracy, or a domestic institution, is no justification, under the law of nations, for illegal or immoral acts.

INTERNATIONAL BELLIGERENT RIGHTS ARE DETERMINED BY THE LAW OF NATIONS.

To determine what are the rights of different nations when making war upon each other, we look only to the law of nations. The peculiar forms or rights of the subjects of one of these war-making parties under their own government give them no rights over their enemy other than those which are sanctioned by international law. In the great tribunal of nations, there is a "higher law" than that which has been framed by either one of them, however sacred to each its own peculiar laws and constitution of government may be.

But while this supreme law is in full force, and is binding on all countries, softening the asperities of war, and guarding the rights of neutrals, it is not conceded that the government of the United States, in a civil war for the suppression of rebellion among its own citizens, is subject to the same limitations as though the rebels were a foreign nation, owing no allegiance to the country.

With this caveat, it will be desirable to state some of the rights of belligerents.

BELLIGERENT RIGHT OF CONFISCATION OF PERSONAL ESTATE.

Either belligerent may seize and confiscate all the property of the enemy, on land or on the sea, including real as well as personal estate.

PRIZE COURTS.

As the property of all nations has an equal right upon the high seas, (the highway of nations,) in order to protect the commerce of neutrals from unlawful interference, it is necessary that ships and cargoes seized on the ocean should be brought before some prize court, that it may be judicially determined whether the captured vessel and cargo were, in whole or in part, enemy's property or contraband of war. The decision of any prize court, according to the law of nations, is conclusive against all the world. Where personal property of the enemy is captured from the enemy, on land, in the enemy's country, no decision of any court is necessary to give a title thereto. Capture passes the title. This is familiar law as administered in the courts of Europe and America.*

TITLE BY CAPTURE.

Some persons have questioned whether title passes in this country by capture or confiscation, by reason of some of the limiting clauses of the constitution; and others have gone so far as to assert that all the proceedings under martial law, such as capturing enemy's property, imprisonment of spies and traitors, and seizures of articles contraband of war, and suspending the *habeas corpus*, are in violation of the constitution, which declares that no man shall be deprived of life, liberty, or

* *Alexander* v. *Duke of Wellington*, 2 Russ. & Mylne, 35. Lord Brougham said that military prize rests upon the same principles of law as prize at sea, though in general no statute passes with respect to it. See 1 Kent, 357.

property without due process of law;* that private property shall not be taken for public use without just compensation; † that unreasonable searches and seizures shall not be made; ‡ that freedom of speech and of the press shall not be abridged; § and that the right of the people to keep and bear arms shall not be infringed. ||

THESE PROVISIONS NOT APPLICABLE TO A STATE OF WAR.

If these rules are applicable to a state of war, then capture of property is illegal, and does not pass a title; no defensive war can be carried on; no rebellion can be suppressed; no invasion can be repelled; the army of the United States, when called into the field, can do no act of hostility. Not a gun can be fired *constitutionally*, because it might deprive a rebel foe of his life without *due process of law*—firing a gun not being deemed "due process of law."

Sect. 4 of Art. IV. says, that "the United States shall guarantee to every State in this Union a republican form of government, and shall protect each of them against invasion, and, on application of the legislature, or of the Executive, when the legislature cannot be convened, against domestic violence."

Art. I. Sect. 8, gives Congress power to declare war, raise and support armies, provide and maintain a navy; to provide for calling forth the militia to execute the laws of the Union, suppress insurrection and repel invasion; to provide for organizing, arming, and disciplining the militia, and for governing such part of them as may be in the service of the United States.

* Constitutional Amendments, Art. V. † Ibid. Art. V.
‡ Ibid. Art. IV. § Ibid. Art. I. || Ibid. Art. II.

If these rules above cited have any application in a time of war, the United States *cannot protect* each of the States from invasion by citizens of other States, nor against domestic violence; nor can the army, or militia, or navy be used for any of the purposes for which the constitution authorizes or requires their employment. If all men have the right to "keep and bear arms," what right has the army of the Union to take them away from rebels? If "no one can constitutionally be deprived of life, liberty, or property, without due process of law," by what right does government seize and imprison traitors? By what right does the army kill rebels in arms, or burn up their military stores? If the only way of dealing constitutionally with rebels in arms is to go to law with them, the President should convert his army into lawyers, justices of the peace, and constables, and serve "summonses to appear and answer to complaints," instead of a summons to surrender. He should send "GREETINGS" instead of sending rifle shot. He should load his caissons with "pleas in abatement and demurrers," instead of thirty-two pound shell and grape shot. In short, he should levy writs of execution, instead of levying war. On the contrary, the commander-in-chief proposes a different application of the due process of law. His summons is, that rebels should lay down their arms; his pleas are batteries and gunboats; his arguments are hot shot, and always "to the point;" and when his fearful execution is "levied on the body," all that is left will be for the undertaker.

TRUE APPLICATION OF THESE CONSTITUTIONAL GUARANTEES.

The clauses which have been cited from the amendments to the constitution were intended as declarations of the rights of peaceful and loyal citizens, and safeguards in the administration of justice by the civil tribunals; but it was necessary, in order to give the government the means of defending itself against domestic or foreign enemies, to maintain its authority and dignity, and to enforce obedience to its laws, that it should have unlimited war powers; and it must not be forgotten that the same authority which provides those safeguards, and guarantees those rights, also imposes upon the President and Congress the duty of so carrying on war as of necessity to supersede and hold in temporary suspense such civil rights as may prove inconsistent with the complete and effectual exercise of such war powers, and of the belligerent rights resulting from them. The rights of war and the rights of peace cannot coexist. One must yield to the other. Martial law and civil law cannot operate at the same time and place upon the same subject matter. Hence the constitution is framed with full recognition of that fact; it protects the citizen in peace and in war; but his rights enjoyed under the constitution, in time of peace are different from those to which he is entitled in time of war.

WHETHER BELLIGERENTS SHALL BE ALLOWED CIVIL RIGHTS UNDER THE CONSTITUTION DEPENDS UPON THE POLICY OF GOVERNMENT.

None of these rights, guaranteed to peaceful citizens, by the constitution belong to them after they have become belligerents against their own government. They thereby forfeit all protection under that sacred charter which they have thus sought to overthrow and destroy. One party to a contract cannot break it and at the same time hold the other to perform it. It is true that if the government elects to treat them as subjects and to hold them liable only to penalties for violating statutes, it must concede to them all the legal rights and privileges which other citizens would have when under similar accusations; and Congress must be limited to the provisions of the constitution in legislation against them as citizens. But the fact that war is waged by these miscreants releases the government from all obligation to make that concession, or to respect the rights to life, liberty, or property of its enemy, because the constitution makes it the duty of the President to prosecute war against them in order to suppress rebellion and repel invasion.

THE CONSTITUTION ALLOWS CONFISCATION.

Nothing in the constitution interferes with the belligerent right of confiscation of enemy property. The right to confiscate is derived from a state of war. It is one of the rights of war. It originates in the principle of self-preservation. It is the means of weakening the enemy and strengthening ourselves. The right of confiscation belongs to the government as the necessary consequence of the power and duty of making war — offensive or defensive. Every capture of enemy ammunition or arms is, in substance, a confiscation, without its formalities. To deny the right of confiscation is to deny the right to make war, or to conquer an enemy.

If authority were needed to support the right of confiscation, it may be found in 3 Dallas, 227; Vat. lib. iii., ch. 8, sect. 188; lib. iii., ch. 9, sect. 161; *Smith* v. *Mansfield*, Cranch, 306–7; *Cooper* v. *Telfair*, 4 Dallas; *Brown* v. *U. S.*, 8 Cranch, 110, 228, 229.

The following extract is from 1 Kent's Com., p. 59: —

"But however strong the current of authority in favor of the modern and milder construction of the rule of national law on this subject, the point seems to be no longer open for discussion in this country; and it has become definitively settled in favor of the ancient and sterner rule by the Supreme Court of the United States. *Brown* v. *United States*, 8 Cranch, 110; ibid. 228, 229.

"The effect of war on British property found in the United States on land, at the commencement of the war, was learnedly discussed and thoroughly considered in the case of Brown, and the Circuit Court of the United States at Boston decided as upon a settled rule of the law of nations, that the goods of the enemy found in the country, and all vessels and cargoes found afloat in our ports at the commencement of hostilities, were liable to seizure and confiscation; and the exercise of the right vested in the discretion of the sovereign of the nation.

"When the case was brought up on appeal before the Supreme Court of the United States, the broad principle was assumed that war gave to the sovereign the full right to take the persons and confiscate the property of the enemy wherever found; and that the mitigations of this rigid rule, which the wise and humane policy of modern times had introduced into practice, might, more or less, affect the exercise of the right, but could not impair the right itself.

"Commercial nations have always considerable property in possession of their neighbors; and when war breaks out, the question, What shall be done with enemy property found in the country? is one rather of policy than of law, and is one properly addressed to the consideration of the legislature, and not to the courts of law.

"The strict right of confiscation of that species of property existed in Congress, and without a legislative act authorizing its confiscation it could not be judicially condemned; and the act of Congress of 1812 declaring war against Great Britain was not such an act. Until some statute directly applying to the subject be passed, the property would continue under the protection of the law, and might be claimed by the British owner at the restoration of peace.

"Though this decision established the right contrary to much of modern authority and practice, yet a great point was gained over the rigor and violence of the ancient doctrine, by making the exercise of the right depend upon a special act of Congress."

From the foregoing authorities, it is evident that the

government has a right, as a belligerent power, to capture or to confiscate any and all the personal property of the enemy; that there is nothing in the constitution which limits or controls the exercise of that right; and that capture in war, or confiscation by law, passes a complete title to the property taken; and that, if *judicial* condemnation of enemy property be sought, in order to pass the title to it by formal decree of courts, by mere seizure, and without capture, the confiscation must have been declared by act of Congress, a mere declaration of war not being *ex vi termini* sufficient for that purpose. The army of the Union, therefore, have the right, according to the law of nations, and of the constitution, to obtain by capture a legal title to all the personal property of the enemy they get possession of, whether it consist of arms, ammunition, provisions, slaves, or any other thing which the law treats as personal property. No judicial process is necessary to give the government full title thereto, and when once captured, the government may dispose of the property as absolute owner thereof, in the same manner as though the title passed by bill of sale: and Congress have plenary authority to pass such confiscation laws against belligerent enemies as they deem for the public good.

MILITARY GOVERNMENT UNDER MARTIAL LAW.

In addition to the right of *confiscating personal property* of the enemy, a state of war also confers upon the government other not less important belligerent rights, and among them, the right to seize and hold conquered territory by military force, and of instituting and maintaining military government over it, thereby suspending in part, or in the whole, the ordinary civil administration. The exercise of this right has been sanctioned by the decision of the Supreme Court of the United States, in the case of California.* And it is founded upon well-established doctrines of the law of nations. Without the right to make laws and administer justice in conquered territory, the inhabitants would be plunged into anarchy. The old government being overthrown, and no new one being established, there would be none to whom allegiance would be due — none to restrain lawlessness, none to secure to any persons any civil rights whatever. Hence, from the necessity of the case, the conqueror has power to establish a quasi military civil administration of government for the protection of the innocent, the restraint of the wicked, and the security of that conquest for which war has been waged.

It is under this power of holding and establishing military rule over conquered territory, that all provisional governments are instituted by conquerors. The President, as commander-in-chief, has formally appointed Andrew Johnson governor of Tennessee, with all the powers, duties, and functions pertaining to that office, during the pleasure of the President, or until the *loyal* inhabitants of that State shall organize a civil government in accordance with the constitution of the United States. To legalize these powers and duties, it became expedient to give him a military position; hence he was nominated as a brigadier general, and his nomination was confirmed by the Senate. Mr. Stanley acts as provisional military governor of North Carolina, under similar authority. All acts of military government which are within the scope of their authority, are as legal and constitutional as any other military

* *Cross* v. *Harrison*, 16 How. 164.

proceeding. Hence any section of this country, which, having joined in a general rebellion, shall have been *subdued* and conquered by the military forces of the United States, may be subjected to military government, and the rights of citizens in those districts are subject to martial law, so long as the war lasts. Whatever of their rights of property are *lost* in and by the war, are lost forever. No citizen, whether loyal or rebel, is deprived of any right guaranteed to him in the constitution by reason of his subjection to *martial law,* because *martial law,* when in force, is *constitutional law.* The people of the United States, through their lawfully chosen commander-in-chief, have the constitutional right to seize and hold the territory of a belligerent enemy, and to govern it by martial law, thereby superseding the local government of the place, and all rights which rebels might have had as citizens of the United States, if they had not violated the laws of the land by making war upon the country.

By martial law, loyal citizens may be for a time debarred from enjoying the rights they would be entitled to in time of peace. Individual rights must always be held subject to the exigencies of national safety.

In war, when *martial law is in force,* the laws of war are the laws which the constitution expressly authorizes and requires to be enforced. The constitution, when it calls into action martial law, for the time changes *civil* rights, or rights which the citizen would be entitled to in peace, because the rights of persons in one of these cases are totally incompatible with the obligations of persons in the other. Peace and war cannot exist together; the laws of peace and of war cannot operate together; the rights and procedures of peaceful times are incompatible with those of war. It is an obvious but pernicious error to suppose that in a *state of war*, the rules of martial law, and the consequent modification of the rights, duties, and obligations of citizens, private and public, are not *authorized* strictly under the *constitution*. And among the rights of martial law, none is more familiar than that of seizing and establishing a military government over territory taken from the enemy; and the duty of thus protecting such territory is imperative, since the United States are obligated to guarantee to each State a republican form of government.* That form of government having been overthrown by force, the country must take such steps, military and civil, as may tend to restore it to the loyal citizens of that State, if there be any; and if there be no persons who will submit to the constitution and laws of the United States, it is their duty to hold that State by military power, and under military rule, until loyal citizens shall appear there in sufficient numbers to entitle them to receive back into their own hands the local government.

A SEVERE RULE OF BELLIGERENT LAW.

"Property of persons residing in the enemy's country is deemed, in law, hostile, and subject to condemnation without any evidence as to the opinions or predilections of the owner." If he be the subject of a neutral, or a citizen of one of the belligerent States, and has expressed no disloyal sentiments towards his country, still his residence in the enemy's country impresses upon his property, engaged in commerce and found upon the ocean, a hostile character, and subjects it to

* Constitution, Art. IV., Sect. 4., Cl. 1.

condemnation. This familiar principle of law is sanctioned in the highest courts of England and of the United States, and has been decided to apply to cases of *civil* as well as of foreign war.*

Thus personal property of every kind, ammunition, provisions, contraband, or slaves, may be lawfully seized, whether of *loyal* or *disloyal* citizens, and is by law *presumed hostile,* and liable to *condemnation,* if *captured within the rebellious districts.* This right of seizure and condemnation is harsh, as all the proceedings of war are harsh, in the extreme, but it is nevertheless lawful. It would be harsh to kill in battle a loyal citizen who, having been impressed into the ranks of the rebels, is made to fight against his country; yet it is lawful to do so.

Against all persons in arms, and against all property situated and seized in rebellious districts, the laws of war give the President full belligerent rights; and when the army and navy are once lawfully called out, there are no limits to the war-making power of the President, other than the law of nations, and such rules as Congress may pass for their regulation.

"The statute of 1807, chap. 39," says a learned judge,† "provides that whenever it is lawful for the President to call forth the militia to suppress an insurrection, he may employ the land and naval forces for that purpose. The authority to use the army is thus expressly confirmed, but the *manner* in which they are to be used is not prescribed. That is left to the discretion of the President, guided by the usages and principles of civilized war."

* *The Venus,* 8 Cranch Rep.; *The Hoop,* 1 Robinson, 196,—and cases there cited. *The Amy Warwick,* opinion of Judge Sprague.

† Judge Sprague.

As a matter of expediency, Congress may direct that *no* property of *loyal citizens*, residing in *disloyal* States, should be seized by military force, without compensation. This is an act of grace, which, though not required by the *laws of war*, may well be granted. The commander-in-chief may also grant the same indulgence. But the military commanders are always at liberty to seize, in an enemy's country, whatever property they deem necessary for the sustenance of troops, or military stores, whether it is the property of friend or enemy; it being usual, however, to pay for all that is taken from friends. These doctrines have been carried into effect in Missouri.

The President having adopted the policy of protecting loyal citizens wherever they may be found, all seizure of their property, and all interference with them, have so far been forborne. But it should be understood that such forbearance is optional, not compulsory. It is done from a sense of justice and humanity, not because law or constitution render it inevitable. And this forbearance is not likely to be carried to such an extent as to endanger the success of the armies of the Union, nor to despoil them of the legitimate fruits of victory over rebels.

CIVIL RIGHTS OF LOYAL CITIZENS IN LOYAL DISTRICTS ARE MODIFIED BY THE EXISTENCE OF WAR.

While war is raging, many of the rights held sacred by the constitution — rights which cannot be violated by any acts of Congress — may and must be suspended and held in abeyance. If this were not so, the government might itself be destroyed; the army and navy might be sacrificed, and one part of the constitution would NULLIFY the rest.

If *freedom of speech* cannot be suppressed, spies cannot be caught, imprisoned, and hung.

If *freedom of the press* cannot be interfered with, all our military plans may be betrayed to the enemy.

If no man can be *deprived of life without trial by jury*, a soldier cannot slay the enemy in battle.

If *enemy's property* cannot be taken without "due process of law," how can the soldier disarm his foe and seize his weapons?

If no person can be arrested, sentenced, and shot, without *trial by jury* in the county or State where his crime is alleged to have been committed, how can a *deserter be shot*, or a *spy be hung*, or an *enemy be taken prisoner?*

It has been said that "*amidst arms* the *laws are silent*." It would be more just to say, that while war rages, the *rights*, which in peace are sacred, must and do give way to the higher right — the right of *public safety* — the right which the COUNTRY, *the whole country, claims* to be protected from its enemies, domestic and foreign — from spies, from conspirators, and from traitors. The sovereign and almost dictatorial powers — existing only in actual war; ending when war ends — to be used in self-defence, and to be laid down when the occasion has passed, are, while they last, as *lawful*, as *constitutional*, as *sacred*, as the administration of justice by judicial courts in times of peace. They may be dangerous; war itself is dangerous; but danger does not make them *unconstitutional*. If the commander-in-chief orders the army to seize the arms and ammunition of the enemy; to capture their persons; to shell out their batteries; to hang spies or shoot deserters; to destroy the armed enemy in open battle; to send traitors to forts and prisons; to stop the press from aiding and comforting the enemy by betraying our military plans; to arrest within our lines, or wherever they can be seized, persons against whom there is reasonable evidence of their having aided or abetted the rebels, or of intending so to do, — the pretension that in so doing he is violating the constitution is not only erroneous, but it is a plea in behalf of treason. To set up the rules of civil administration as overriding and controlling the laws of war, is to aid and abet the enemy. It falsifies the clear meaning of the constitution, which not only gives the power, but makes it the plain duty of the President, to go to war with the enemy of his country. And the restraints to which he is subject *when in war*, are not to be found in the municipal regulations, which can be administered only in peace, but in the laws and usages of nations regulating the conduct of war.

BELLIGERENT RIGHT TO CONFISCATE ENEMY'S REAL ESTATE.

The *belligerent right* of the government to confiscate *enemy's real estate, situated in this country*, can hardly admit of a question. The title to no inconsiderable part of the real estate in each of the original States of the Union, rests upon the validity of confiscation acts, passed by our ancestors against loyal adherents to the crown. Probably none of these States failed to pass and apply these laws. English and American acts of confiscation were recognized by the laws of both countries, and their operation modified by treaties; their *validity never was denied.* The *only* authority which either of the States or colonies ever had for passing such laws was derived from the fact that they were *belligerents.*

It will be observed that the question as to the belligerent right to confiscate enemy's real estate situated in the United States, is somewhat different from the question whether in conquering a foreign country it will be lawful to confiscate the private real estate of the enemy.

It is *unusual,* in case of *conquest* of a foreign country, for the conqueror to do more than to displace its sovereign, and assume dominion over the country. On a *mere* change of *sovereignty* of the country, it would be harsh and severe to confiscate the private property and annul the private rights of citizens generally. And *mere* conquest of a country does not *of itself* operate as confiscation of enemy's property; nor does the cession of a country by one nation to another destroy private rights of property, or operate as confiscation of personal or real estate.* So it was held by the Supreme Court in the case of the transfer by treaty of Florida to the United States; but it was specially provided in that treaty that private property should not be interfered with. The forbearance of a conqueror from confiscating the entire property of a conquered people is usually founded in good policy, as well as in humanity. The object of foreign conquest is to acquire a permanent addition to the power and territory of the conqueror. This object would be defeated by stripping his subjects of every thing. The case is very different where confiscation will only break up a nest of traitors, and drive them away from a country they have betrayed.

Suppose that certain Englishmen owned large tracts

* *United States* v. *Juan Richmond,* 7 Peters, 51.

of real estate in either of the United States or territories thereof, and war should break out; would any one doubt the right of Congress to pass a law confiscating such estate?

The laws of nations allow either belligerent to seize and appropriate whatever property of the enemy it can gain possession of; and, of all descriptions of property which government could safely permit to be owned or occupied by an alien enemy, real estate within its own dominion would be the last.

No distinction can be properly or legally made between the different kinds of enemy property, whether real, personal, or mixed, so far as regards their liability to confiscation by the war power. Lands, money, slaves, debts, may and have been subject to this liability. The methods of appropriating and holding them are different — the result is the same. And, considering the foundation of the right, the object for which it is to be exercised, and the effects resulting from it, there is nothing in law, or in reason, which would indicate why one can and the other cannot be taken away from the enemy.

In *Brown* v. *United States*, 8 Cranch, p. 123, the Supreme Court of the United States say, —

"Respecting the power of government, no doubt is entertained. That war gives to the sovereign the full right to take the persons and confiscate the property of the enemy, wherever found, is conceded. The mitigations of this rule, which the humane and wise policy of modern times has introduced into practice, will more or less affect the exercise of this right, but cannot impair the right itself — that remains undiminished; and when the sovereign authority shall choose to bring it into operation, the judicial department must give effect to its will."

"It may be considered," they say, "as the opinion of all who have written on the *jus belli*, that war gives the *right* to confiscate," &c.

Chancellor Kent says, —

"When war is duly declared, it is not merely a war between this and the adverse government in their political characters. Every man is, in judgment of law, a party to the acts of his own government, and a war between the government of two nations is a war between all the individuals of the one and all the individuals of which the other nation is composed. Government is the representative of the will of the people, and acts for the whole society. This is the theory of all governments, and the best writers on the law of nations concur in the doctrine, that when the sovereign of a state declares war against another sovereign, it implies that the whole nation declares war, and that all the subjects of the one are enemies to all the subjects of the other."

"Very important consequences concerning the obligations of subjects are deducible from this principle. When hostilities have commenced, the first objects that present themselves for detention and capture are the persons and property of the enemy found within the territory on the breaking out of war. According to strict authority, a state has a right to deal as an enemy with persons and property so found within its power, and to confiscate the property and detain the persons as prisoners of war." *

We thus see, that by the law of nations, by the practice of our own States, by the decisions of courts, by the highest authority of legal writers, and by the deductions of reason, there can be no question of the constitutional right of confiscation of enemy real estate of which we may gain possession. And the legal presumption that real estate situated in rebellious districts is enemy property, would seem to be as well founded as it is in case of personal property.†

It is for the government to decide how it shall use its belligerent right of confiscation. The number of slaveholders in the rebellious States, who

* 1 Kent's Com., p. 55. See also Grotius, B. III. ch. 3, sect. 9; ch. 4, sect. 8. Burlamaqui, Part IV. ch. 4, sect. 20. Vattel, B. III. ch. 5, sect. 70.

† See page 57.

are the principal land owners in that region, and who are the chief authors and supporters of this rebellion, constitute, all told, less than *one in one hundred and twenty eight* of the people of the United States, and less than *one fiftieth* part of the inhabitants of their own districts, being far less in proportion to the whole population of the country than the *old tories* in the time of the revolution were to the colonists.*

* In confirmation of these views of the War Powers of Congress, see the chapter on the War Powers of the President, and NOTES thereon.

CHAPTER III.

WAR POWER OF THE PRESIDENT TO EMANCIPATE SLAVES.

THE power of the President, as commander-in-chief of the army and navy of the United States, when in actual service, to emancipate the slaves of any belligerent section of the country, if such a measure becomes necessary to save the government from destruction, is not, it is presumed, denied by any respectable authority.*

WHY THE POWER EXISTS.

The liberation of slaves is looked upon as a means of embarrassing or weakening the enemy, or of strengthening the military power of our army. If slaves be treated as contraband of war, on the ground that they may be used by their masters to aid in prosecuting war, as employees upon military works, or as laborers furnishing by their industry the means of carrying on hostilities; or if they be treated as, in law, belligerents, following the legal condition of their owners; or if they be deemed loyal subjects having a just claim upon the government to be released from their obligations to give aid and service to disloyal and belligerent masters, in order that they may be free to perform their higher duty of allegiance and loyalty to the United States; or if they be regarded as subjects

* It has been shown in a previous chapter that the government has a right to treat *rebels* either as *belligerents* or as subjects, and to subject them to the severities of international belligerent law.

of the United States, liable to do military duty; or if they be made citizens of the United States, and soldiers; or if the authority of the masters over their slaves is the means of aiding and comforting the enemy, or of throwing impediments in the way of the government, or depriving it of such aid and assistance in successful prosecution of the war, as slaves would and could afford, if released from the control of the enemy, — or if releasing the slaves would embarrass the enemy, and make it more difficult for them to collect and maintain large armies; in either of these cases, the taking away of these slaves from the "aid and service" of the enemy, and putting them to the aid and service of the United States, is justifiable as an act of war. The ordinary way of depriving the enemy of slaves is by declaring emancipation.

THE PRESIDENT IS THE SOLE JUDGE.

"It belongs exclusively to the President to judge when the exigency arises in which he has authority, under the constitution, to call forth the militia, and his decision is conclusive on all other persons." *

The constitution confers on the Executive, when in actual war, full belligerent powers. The emancipation of enemy's slaves is a belligerent right. It belongs exclusively to the President, as commander-in-chief, to judge whether he shall exercise his belligerent right to emancipate slaves in those parts of the country which are in rebellion. If exercised in fact, and while the war lasts, his act of emancipation is conclusive and

* Such is the language of Chief Justice Taney, in delivering the opinion of the Supreme Court, in *Martin* v. *Mott*, 12 Wheaton, 19.

binding forever on all the departments of government, and on all persons whatsoever.

POWERS OF THE PRESIDENT NOT INCONSISTENT WITH POWERS OF CONGRESS TO EMANCIPATE SLAVES.

The right of the Executive to strike this blow against his enemy does not deprive Congress of the concurrent right or duty to emancipate enemy's slaves, if in *their judgment* a civil act for that purpose is required by public welfare and common defence, for the purpose of aiding and giving effect to such war measures as the commander-in-chief may adopt.

The military authority of the President is not incompatible with the peace or war powers of Congress; but both coexist, and may be exercised upon the same subject. Thus, when the army captures a regiment of soldiers, the legislature may pass laws relating to the captives. So may Congress destroy slavery by abolishing the laws which sustain it, while the commander of the army may destroy it by capture of slaves, by proclamation, or by other means.

IS LIBERATION OF ENEMY'S SLAVES A BELLIGERENT RIGHT?

This is the chief inquiry on this branch of the subject. To answer it we must appeal to the law of nations, and learn whether there is any commanding authority which forbids the use of an engine so powerful and so formidable — an engine which may grind to powder the disloyalty of rebels in arms, while it clears the avenue to freedom for four millions of Americans. It is only the law of nations that can decide this question, because the constitution, having given authority to government to make war, has placed no limit whatever to the war powers. There is, therefore, no legal control over the war powers except the law of nations, and no moral control except the usage of modern civilized belligerents.

THE LAW OF NATIONS SANCTIONS EMANCIPATION OF ENEMY'S SLAVES.

It is in accordance with the law of nations and with the practice of civilized belligerents in modern times, to liberate enemy's slaves in time of war by military power. In the revolutionary war, England exercised that unquestioned right by not less than three of her military commanders — Sir Henry Clinton, Lord Dunmore, and Lord Cornwallis. That General Washington recognized and feared Lord Dunmore's appeal to the slaves, is shown by his letter on that subject.

"His strength," said Washington, "will increase as a snow-ball by rolling faster and faster, if some expedient cannot be hit upon to convince the slaves and servants of the impotency of his designs."

The right to call the slaves of colonists to the aid of the British arms was expressly admitted by Jefferson, in his letter to Dr. Gordon. In writing of the injury done to his estates by Cornwallis, he uses the following language: —

"He destroyed all my growing crops and tobacco; he burned all my barns, containing the same articles of last year. Having first taken what corn he wanted, he used, *as was to be expected*, all my stock of cattle, sheep, and hogs, for the sustenance of his army, and carried off all the horses capable of service. *He carried off also about thirty slaves. Had this been to give them freedom, he would have done right.* . . . From an estimate made at the time on the best information I could collect, I suppose the State of Virginia lost under Lord Cornwallis's hands, that year, about thirty thousand slaves."

Great Britain, for the second time, used the same right against us in the war of 1812. Her naval and military commanders invited the slaves, by public proclamations, to repair to their standard, promising them freedom.* The slaves who went over to them were liberated, and were carried away contrary to the express terms of the treaty of Ghent, in which it was stipulated that they should not be carried away. England preferred to become liable for a breach of the treaty rather than to break faith with the fugitives. Indemnity for this violation of contract was demanded and refused. The question was referred to the decision of the Emperor of Russia, as arbitrator, who decided that indemnity should be paid by Great Britain, not because she had violated the law of nations in emancipating slaves, but because she had broken the terms of the treaty.

In the arguments submitted to the referee, the British government broadly asserted the belligerent right of liberating enemy's slaves, even if they were treated as private property. Mr. Middleton was instructed by Mr. J. Q. Adams, then, in 1820, Secretary of State, to deny that right, and to present reasons for that denial. But that in this instance he acted in obedience to the instructions of the President and cabinet, and against his own opinions on the law of nations, is shown by his subsequent statement in Congress to that effect.† The question of international law was left undecided by the Emperor; but the assertion of England, that it is a

* For Admiral Cochrane's Proclamation, instigating the slaves to desert their masters, see Niles's Register, vol. vi. p. 242.

† "It was utterly against my judgment and wishes; but I was obliged to submit, and prepared the requisite despatches." See Congressional Globe, XXVII. Cong., 2d sess., 1841–2; vol. ii. p. 424.

legitimate exercise of belligerent rights to liberate enemy's slaves, — a right which had previously been enforced by her against the colonies, and by France against her, and again by her against the United States, — was entitled to great weight, as a reiterated and authentic reaffirmance of the well-settled doctrine.

In speeches before the House of Representatives on the 25th of May, 1836, on the 7th of June, 1841, and on the 14th and 15th of April, 1842, Mr. Adams explained and asserted in the amplest terms the powers of Congress, and the authority of the President, to free enemy's slaves, as a legitimate act of war.* Thus leading statesmen of England and America have concurred in the opinion that emancipation is a belligerent right.

St. Domingo, in 1793, contained more than five hundred thousand negroes, with many mulattoes and whites, and was held as a province of France. Intestine commotions had raged for nearly three years between the whites and mulattoes, in which the negroes had remained neutral. The Spaniards having effected an alliance with the slaves who had revolted in 1791, invaded the island and occupied several important military points. England, also, was making a treaty with the planters to invade the country; and thus the possession seemed about to be wrested from France by the efforts of one or the other of its two bitterest foes. One thousand French soldiers, a few mulattoes and loyal slaveholders, were all the force which could be mustered in favor of the government, for the protection of this precious island, situated so far away from France.

* For extracts from these speeches, see *postea*.

Sonthonax and Polverel, the French commissioners, on the 29th of August, 1793, issued a proclamation, under martial law, wherein they declared all the slaves free, and thereby brought them over *en masse* to the support of the government. The English troops landed three weeks afterwards, and were repulsed principally by the slave army.

On the 4th of February, 1794, the National Convention of France confirmed the act of the commissioners, and also abolished slavery in the other French colonies.

In June, 1794, Toussaint L'Ouverture, a colored man, admitted by military critics to be one of the great generals of modern times, having until then fought in favor of Spain, brought his army of five thousand colored troops to the aid of France, forced entrance into the chief city of the island in which the French troops were beleaguered, relieved his allies, and offered himself and his army to the service of that government, which had guaranteed to them their freedom. From that hour the fortunes of the war changed. The English were expelled from the island in 1798; the Spaniards also gave it up; and in 1801 Toussaint proclaimed the republic in the Spanish portion of the island which had been ceded to France by the treaty of 1795; thus extending the practical operation of the decree of emancipation over the whole island, and liberating one hundred thousand more persons who had been slaves of Spaniards.

The island was put under martial law; the planters were recalled by Toussaint, and permitted to hire their former slaves; and his government was enforced by military power; and from that time until 1802, the progress of the people in commerce, industry, and general prosperity was rapid and satisfactory. But in 1802 the influence of emigrant planters, and of the Empress Josephine, a creole of Martinique, induced Napoleon to send a large army to the island, to reëstablish the slave trade and slavery in all the other islands except St. Domingo, with the design of restoring slavery there after he should have conquered it. But war, sickness, and disasters broke up his forces, and the treacherous Frenchmen met the due reward of their perfidy, and were, in 1804, totally driven from the island. The independence of St. Domingo was actually established in 1804. The independence of Hayti was recognized by the United States in 1862.

From this brief outline it is shown, that France recognizes the right, under martial law, to emancipate the slaves of an enemy — having asserted and exercised that right in the case of St. Domingo.* And the slaves thus liberated have retained their liberty, and compose, at this day, the principal population of a government who have entered into diplomatic relations with the United States.

In Colombia slavery was abolished, first by the Spanish General Morillo, and secondly by the American General Bolivar. "It was abolished," says John Quincy Adams, "by virtue of a military command given at the head of the army, and its abolition continues to this day. It was abolished by the laws of war, and not by the municipal enactments; the power was exercised

* For the decree of the French Assembly, see *Choix de Rapports — Opinions et Discours prononcés à la Tribune Nationale depuis* 1789. Paris, 1821, t. xiv. p. 425. — See *Abolition d'Esclavage, (Colonies Francaises,) par Augustin Cochin.* Paris, 1861. Vol. i. pp. 14, 15, &c.

by military commanders, under instructions, of course, from their respective governments."

AUTHORITY AND USAGE CONFIRM THE RIGHT.

It may happen that when belligerents on both sides hold slaves, neither will deem it expedient, through fear of retaliation, to liberate the slaves of his adversary; but considerations of policy do not affect questions of international rights; and forbearance to exercise a power does not prove its non-existence. While no authority among eminent ancient writers on the subject has been found to deny the right of emancipation, the fact that England, France, Spain, and the South American republics have actually freed the slaves of their enemies, conclusively shows that the law and practice of modern civilized nations sanction that right.

HOW FAR THE GOVERNMENT OF THE UNITED STATES UNDER FORMER ADMINISTRATIONS HAVE SANCTIONED THE BELLIGERENT RIGHT OF EMANCIPATING SLAVES OF LOYAL AND OF DISLOYAL CITIZENS.

The government of the United States, in 1814, recognized the right of their military officers, in time of war, to appropriate to public use the slaves of loyal citizens without compensation therefor; also, in 1836, the right to reward slaves who have performed public service, by giving freedom to them and to their families; also, in 1838, the principle that slaves of loyal citizens, captured in war, should be emancipated, and not returned to their masters; and that slaves escaping to the army of the United States should be treated as prisoners of war, and not as property of their masters. These propositions are supported by the cases of General Jackson, General Jessup, General Taylor, and General Gaines.

"In December, 1814," says a distinguished writer and speaker, "General Jackson impressed a large number of slaves at and near New Orleans, and set them at work erecting defences, behind which his troops won such glory on the 8th of January, 1815. The masters remonstrated. Jackson disregarded their remonstrances, and kept the slaves at work until many of them were killed by the enemy's shot; yet his action was approved by Mr. Madison, the cabinet, and by the Congress, which has ever refused to pay the masters for their losses. In this case, the masters were professedly friends to the government; and yet our Presidents, and cabinets, and generals have not hesitated to emancipate their slaves, whenever in time of war it was supposed to be for the interest of the country to do so. This was done in the exercise of the war power to which Mr. Adams referred, and for which he had the most abundant authority."

"In 1836 General Jessup engaged several fugitive slaves to act as guides and spies, agreeing, if they would serve the government faithfully, to secure to them the freedom of themselves and families. They fulfilled their engagement in good faith. The general gave them their freedom, and sent them to the west. Mr. Van Buren's administration sanctioned the contract, and Mr. Tyler's administration approved the proceeding of the general in setting the slaves and their families free."

The writer above quoted says, —

"Louis, the slave of a man named Pacheco, betrayed Major Dade's battalion, in 1836, and when he had witnessed their massacre, he joined the enemy. Two years subsequently he was captured. Pacheco claimed him; General Jessup said if he had time, he would try him before a court martial and hang him, but would not deliver him to any man. He, however, sent him west, and the fugitive slave became a free men. General Jessup reported his action to the War Department, and Mr. Van Buren, then President, with his cabinet, approved it. Pacheco then appealed to Congress, asking that body to pay him for the loss of his slave. The House of Representatives voted against the bill, which was rejected. All concurred in the opinion that General Jessup did right in emancipating the slave, instead of returning him to his master.

"In 1838 General Taylor captured a number of negroes said to be fugitive slaves. Citizens of Florida, learning what had been done, immediately gathered around his camp, intending to secure the slaves who had escaped from them. General Taylor told them that he had no prisoners but 'prisoners of war.' The claimants then desired to look at them, in order to determine whether he was holding their slaves as prisoners. The veteran warrior replied that no man should examine his prisoners for such a purpose; and he ordered them to depart. This action, being reported to the War Department, was approved by the Executive. The slaves, however, were sent west, and set free.

"In 1838 many fugitive slaves and Indians, captured in Florida, had been ordered to be sent west of the Mississippi. Some of them were claimed at New Orleans by their owners, under legal process. General Gaines, commander of the military district, refused to deliver them up to the sheriff, and appeared in court and stated his own defence.

"His grounds of defence were, 'that these men, women, and children were captured in war, and held as prisoners of war; that as commander of that military department he held them subject only to the order of the national Executive; that he could recognize no other power in time of war, or by the laws of war, as authorized to take prisoners from his possession. He asserted that in time of war all slaves were belligerents as much as their masters. The slave men cultivate the earth, and supply provisions. The women cook the food and nurse the sick, and contribute to the maintenance of the war, often more than the same number of males. The slave children equally contribute whatever they are able to the support of the war. The military officer, he said, can enter into no judicial examination of the claim of one man to the bone and muscle of another, as property; nor could he, as a military officer, know what the laws of Florida were while engaged in maintaining the federal government by force of arms. In such case he could only be guided by the laws of war, and whatever may be the laws of any State, they must yield to the safety of the federal government. He sent the slaves west, and they became free.'"*

On the 26th of May, 1836, in a debate in the House of Representatives upon the joint resolution for *distributing rations* to the distressed fugitives from Indian hostilities

* This defence of General Gaines may be found in House Document No. 225 of the 2d session of the 25th Congress.

in the states of Alabama and Georgia, JOHN QUINCY ADAMS expressed the following opinions: —

"Sir, in the authority given to Congress by the constitution of the United States to *declare war*, all the powers incidental to war are, by necessary implication, conferred upon the *government* of the United States. Now, the powers incidental to war are derived, not from their internal municipal source, *but from the laws and usages of nations.*

"There are, then, Mr. Chairman, in the *authority of Congress and of the Executive, two classes of powers, altogether different in their nature, and often incompatible with each other — the war power and the peace power.* The peace power is limited by regulations and restricted by provisions prescribed within the Constitution itself. *The war power* is limited only by the laws and usages of nations. This power is tremendous; *it is strictly constitutional, but it breaks down every barrier so anxiously erected for the protection of liberty, of property, and of life.* This, sir, is the power which authorizes you to pass the resolution now before you, and, in my opinion, no other."

After an interruption, Mr. Adams went on to say, —

"There are, indeed, powers of peace conferred upon Congress which also come within the scope and jurisdiction of the laws of nations, such as the negotiation of treaties of amity and commerce, the interchange of public ministers and consuls, and all the personal and social intercourse between the individual inhabitants of the United States and foreign nations, and the Indian tribes, which require the interposition of any law. *But the powers of war are all* regulated by the laws of nations, and *are subject to no other limitation.* . . . It was upon this principle that I voted *against* the resolution reported by the slavery committee, 'that Congress possess no constitutional authority to interfere, *in any way*, with the institution of slavery in any of the States of this confederacy,' to which resolution most of those with whom I usually concur, and even my own colleagues in this house, gave their assent. *I do not admit that there is, even among the peace powers of Congress, no such authority; but in war, there are many ways by which Congress not only have the authority, but* ARE BOUND TO INTERFERE WITH THE INSTITUTION OF SLAVERY IN THE STATES. The *existing law prohibiting the importation of slaves* into the United States from foreign countries is itself an *interference with the insti-*

tution of slavery in the States. It was so considered by the founders of the constitution of the United States, in which it was stipulated that Congress should not interfere, in that way, with the institution, prior to the year 1808.

"During the late war with Great Britain, the military and naval commanders of that nation issued proclamations inviting the slaves to repair to their standard, with promises of freedom and of settlement in some of the British colonial establishments. This surely was an interference with the institution of slavery in the States. By the treaty of peace, Great Britian stipulated to evacuate all the forts and places in the United States, without carrying away any slaves. If the government of the United States had no power to interfere, *in any way*, with the institution of slavery in the States, they would not have had the authority to require this stipulation. It is well known that this engagement was not fulfilled by the British naval and military commanders; that, on the contrary, they did carry away all the slaves whom they had induced to join them, and that the *British government inflexibly refused to restore any of them to their masters;* that a claim of indemnity was consequently instituted in behalf of the owners of the slaves, and was successfully maintained. All that series of transactions was an interference by Congress with the institution of slavery in the States in one way — in the way of protection and support. It was by the institution of slavery alone that the restitution of slaves, enticed by proclamations into the British service, could be claimed as *property.* But for the institution of slavery, the British commanders could neither have allured them to their standard, nor restored them otherwise than as liberated prisoners of war. But for the institution of slavery, there could have been no stipulation that they should not be carried away as property, nor any claim of indemnity for the violation of that engagement."

Mr. Adams goes on to state how the war power may be used: —

"But the war power of Congress over the institution of slavery in the States is yet far more extensive. Suppose the case of a servile war, complicated, as to some extent it is even now, with an Indian war; suppose Congress were called to raise armies, *to supply money from the whole Union to suppress a servile insurrection:* would they have no authority to interfere with the institution of slavery? The issue of a servile war may be disastrous; it may become necessary for the master of the slave to recognize his emancipation by a treaty of peace: can it for an instant be pretended that Congress, in such a contingency, would have no authority to interfere with the institution of slavery, *in any way*, in the States? Why, it would be equivalent to saying that Congress have no constitutional authority to make peace. I suppose a more portentous case, certainly within the bounds of possibility — I would to God I could say, not within the bounds of probability — "

"Do you imagine," he asks, "that your Congress will have no constitutional authority to interfere with the institution of slavery, in any way, in the States of this confederacy? Sir, they must and will interfere with it — perhaps to sustain it by war, perhaps to abolish it by treaties of peace; and they will not only possess the constitutional power so to interfere, but they will be bound in duty to do it, by the express provisions of the constitution itself. From the instant that your slaveholding States become the theatre of a war, *civil, servile, or foreign war*, from that instant the war powers of Congress extend to interference with the institution of slavery, in every way by which it can be interfered with, from a claim of indemnity for slaves taken or destroyed, to the cession of States burdened with slavery to a foreign power."

Extracts from the speech of John Quincy Adams, delivered in the United States House of Representatives, April 14th and 15th, 1842, on war with Great Britain and Mexico: —

"What I say is involuntary, because the subject has been brought into the house from another quarter, as the gentleman himself admits. I would leave that institution to the exclusive consideration and management of the States more peculiarly interested in it, just as long as they can keep within their own bounds. So far, I admit that Congress has no power to meddle with it. As long as they do not step out of their own bounds, and do not put the question to the people of the United States, whose peace, welfare, and happiness are all at stake, so long I will agree to leave them to themselves. But when a member from a free State brings forward certain resolutions, for which, instead of reasoning to disprove his positions, you vote a censure upon him, and that without hearing, it is quite another affair. At the time this was done, I said that, as far as I could understand the resolutions proposed by the gentleman from Ohio, (Mr. Giddings,) there were some of them for which I was ready to vote, and some which I must vote against; and I will now tell this house, my constituents, and the whole of mankind, that the resolution against which I would have voted was that in which he declares that what are called the slave States have the exclusive right of consultation on the subject of slavery. For that resolution I never would vote, because I believe that it is not just, and does not contain constitutional doctrine. I believe that, so long as the slave States are able to sustain their institutions without going abroad or calling upon other parts of the Union to aid them or act on the subject, so long I will consent never to interfere. I have said this, and I repeat it; but if they come to the free States, and say to them, You must help us to keep down our slaves, you must aid us in an insurrection and a civil war, then I say that with that call comes full and plenary power to this house and to the Senate over the whole subject. It is a war power. I say it is a war power; and when your country is actually in war, whether it be a war of invasion or a war of insurrection, Congress has power to carry on the war, and must carry it on, according to the laws of war; and by the laws of war, an invaded country has all its laws and municipal institutions swept by the board, and martial law takes the place of them. This power in Congress has, perhaps, never been called into exercise under the present constitution of the United States. But when the laws of war are in force, what, I ask, is one of those laws? It is this: that when a country is invaded, and two hostile armies are set in martial array, *the commanders of both armies have power to emancipate all the slaves in the invaded territory.* Nor is this a mere theoretic statement. The history of South America shows that the doctrine has been carried into practical execution within the last thirty years. Slavery was abolished in Colombia, first, by the Spanish General Morillo, and, secondly, by the American General Bolivar. It was abolished by virtue of a military command given at the head of the army, and its abolition continues to be law to this day. It was abolished by the laws of war, and not by the municipal enactments; the power was exercised by military commanders, under instructions, of course, from their respective governments. And here I recur again to the example of General Jackson. What are you now about in Congress? You are about passing a grant to refund to General Jackson the amount of a certain fine imposed upon him by a judge, under the laws of the State of Louisiana. You are going to refund him the money, with interest; and this you are going to do because the imposition of the fine was unjust. And why was it unjust? Because General Jackson was acting under the laws of war, and because the moment you place a military commander in a district which is the theatre of war, the laws of war apply to that district.

* * * * * * *

"I might furnish a thousand proofs to show that the pretensions of gentlemen to the sanctity of their municipal institutions under a state of actual invasion and of actual war, whether servile, civil, or foreign, is wholly unfounded, and that the laws of war do, in all such cases, take the precedence. I lay this down as the law of nations. I say that military authority takes, for the time, the place of all municipal institutions, *and slavery among the rest;* and that, under that state of things, so far from its being true that the States where slavery exists have the exclusive management of the subject, not only the President of the United States, but the commander of the army, has power to order the universal emancipation of the slaves. I have given here more in detail a principle which I have asserted on this floor before now, and of which I have no more doubt than that you, sir, occupy that chair. I give it in its development, in order that any gentleman from any part of the Union may, if he thinks proper, deny the truth of the position, and may maintain his denial; not by indignation, not by passion and fury, but by sound and sober reasoning from the laws of nations and the laws of war. And if my position can be answered and refuted, I shall receive the refutation with pleasure; I shall be glad to listen to reason, aside, as I say, from indignation and passion. And if, by the force of reasoning, my understanding can be convinced, I here pledge myself to recant what I have asserted.

"Let my position be answered; let me be told, let my constituents be told, let the people of my State be told, — a State whose soil tolerates not the foot of a slave, — that they are bound by the constitution to a long and toilsome march, under burning summer suns and a deadly southern clime, for the suppression of a servile war; that they are bound to leave their bodies to rot upon the sands of Carolina, to leave their wives widows and their children orphans; that those who cannot march are bound to pour out their treasures while their sons or brothers are pouring out their blood to suppress a servile, combined with a civil or a foreign war; and yet that there exists no power beyond the limits of the slave State where such war is raging to emancipate the slaves. I say, let this be proved — I am open to conviction; but till that conviction comes, I put it forth, not as a dictate of feeling, but as a settled maxim of the laws of nations, that, in such a case, the military supersedes the civil power; and on this account I should have been obliged to vote, as I have said, against one of the resolutions of my excellent friend from Ohio, (Mr. Giddings,) or should at least have required that it be amended in conformity with the constitution of the United States."

CONCLUSION.

It has thus been proved, that by the law and usage of modern civilized nations, confirmed by the judgment of eminent statesmen, and by the former practice of this government, that the President, as commander-in-chief, has the authority, as an act of war, to liberate the slaves of the enemy, that the United States have in former times sanctioned the liberation of slaves even of loyal citizens, by military commanders, in time of war, without compensation therefor; and have deemed slaves captured in war from belligerent subjects as entitled to their freedom.*

* GENERAL WAR POWERS OF THE PRESIDENT. It is not intended in this chapter to explain the *general* war powers of the President. They are principally contained in the Constitution, Art. II. Sect. 1, Cl. 1 and 7; Sect. 2, Cl. 1; Sect. 3, Cl. 1; and in Sect. 1, Cl. 1, and by necessary implication in Art. I. Sect. 9, Cl. 2. By Art. II. Sect. 2, the President is made commander-in-chief of the army and navy of the United States, and of the militia of the several States when called into the service of the United States. This clause gives ample powers of war to the President, when the army and navy are lawfully in "actual service." His military authority is supreme, under the constitution, while governing and regulating the land and naval forces, and treating captures on land and water in accordance with such rules as Congress may have passed in pursuance of Art. I. Sect. 8, Cl. 11, 14. Congress may effectually control the military power, by refusing to vote supplies, or to raise troops, and by impeachment of the President; but for the military movements, and measures essential to overcome the enemy, — for the general conduct of the war, — the President is responsible to and controlled by no other department of government. His duty is to uphold the constitution and enforce the laws, and to respect whatever rights loyal citizens are entitled to enjoy in time of civil war, to the fullest extent that may be consistent with the performance of the military duty imposed on him. The effect of a state of war, in changing or modifying civil rights, has been explained in the preceding chapters.

What is the extent of the military power of the President over the persons and property of citizens at a distance from the seat of war — whether he or the war department may lawfully order the arrest of citizens in loyal states on reasonable proof that they are either enemies or aiding the enemy — or that they are spies or emissaries of rebels sent to gain information for their use, or to discourage enlistments — whether martial law may be extended over such places as the commander deems it necessary to guard, even though distant from any battle field, in order to enable him to prosecute the war effectually — whether the writ of *habeas corpus* may be suspended as to persons under military arrest, by the President, or only by Congress, (on which point judges of the United States courts disagree); whether, in time of war, all citizens are liable to military arrest, on reasonable proof of their aiding or abetting the enemy — or whether they are entitled to practise treason until indicted by some grand jury — thus, for example, whether Jefferson Davis, or General Lee, if found in Boston, could be arrested by military authority and sent to Fort Warren? Whether, in the midst of wide-spread and terrific war, those persons who violate the laws of war and the laws of peace, traitors, spies, emissaries, brigands, bush-whackers, guerrillas, persons in the free States supplying arms and ammunition to the enemy, must all be proceeded against by civil tribunals only, under due forms and precedents of law, by the tardy and ineffectual machinery of arrests by *marshals*, (who can rarely have means of apprehending them,) and of grand *juries*, (who meet twice a year, and could seldom if ever seasonably secure the evidence on which to indict them)? Whether government is not entitled by military power to PREVENT the traitors and spies, by arrest and imprisonment, from doing the intended mischief, as well as to punish them after it is done? Whether war can be carried on successfully, without the power to save the army and navy from being betrayed and destroyed, by *depriving* any citizen temporarily of the power of acting as an enemy, whenever there is reasonable cause to suspect him of being one? Whether these and similar proceedings are, or are not, in violation of any civil rights of citizens under the constitution, are questions to which the answers depend on the construction given to the war powers of the Executive. Whatever any commander-in-chief, in accordance with the usual practice of carrying on war among civilized nations, may order his army and navy to do, is within the *power* of the President to order and to execute, because the constitution, in express terms, gives him the supreme command of both. If he makes war upon a foreign nation, he should be governed by the law of nations; if lawfully engaged in civil war, he may treat his enemies as subjects and as belligerents.

The constitution provides that the government and regulation of the land and naval forces, and the treatment of captures, should be according to law; but it imposes, in express terms, no other qualification of the war power of the President. It does not prescribe any territorial limits, within the United States, to which his military operations shall be restricted; nor to which the picket guard, or military guards (sometimes called *provost marshals*) shall be confined. It does not exempt any person making war upon the country, or aiding and comforting the enemy, from being *captured*, or arrested, wherever he may be found, whether within or out of the lines of any division of the army. It does not provide that public enemies, or their abettors, shall find safe asylum in any part of the United States where military power can reach them. It requires the President, as an executive magistrate, in time of peace to see that the laws existing in time of peace are faithfully executed — and as commander-in-chief, in time of war, to see that the laws of war are executed. In doing both duties he is strictly obeying the constitution.

CHAPTER IV.

BILLS OF ATTAINDER.

AFTER the authority of government shall have been reëstablished over the rebellious districts, measures may be taken to punish individual criminals.

The popular sense of outraged justice will embody itself in more or less stringent legislation against those who have brought civil war upon us. It would be surprising if extreme severity were not demanded by the supporters of the Union in all sections of the country. Nothing short of a general bill of attainder, it is presumed, will fully satisfy some of the loyal people of the slave States.

BILLS OF ATTAINDER IN ENGLAND.

By these statutes, famous in English political history, tyrannical governments have usually inflicted their severest revenge upon traitors. The irresistible power of law has been evoked to annihilate the criminal, as a citizen of that State whose majesty he had offended, and whose existence he had assailed. His life was terminated with horrid tortures; his blood was corrupted, and his estates were forfeited to the king. While still living, he was deemed, in the language of the law, as "*civiliter mortuus.*"

PUNISHMENT BY ATTAINDER.

The refined cruelty which characterized the punishment of treason, according to the common law of England, would have been discreditable to the barbarism of North American savages in the time of the Georges, and has since been equalled only by some specimens of chivalry in the secession army. The mode of executing these unfortunate political offenders was this: —

1. The culprit was required to be dragged on the ground or over the pavement to the gallows; he could not be allowed, by law, to walk or ride. Blackstone says, that *by connivance*, at last ripened into law, he was allowed to be dragged upon a hurdle, to prevent the extreme torment of being dragged on the ground or pavement.

2. To be hanged by the neck, and then cut down alive.

3. His entrails to be taken out and burned while he was yet alive.

4. His head to be cut off.

5. His body to be divided into four parts.

6. His head and quarters to be at the king's disposal.*

Blackstone informs us that these directions were, in former times, literally and studiously executed. Judge Story observes, they "indicate at once a savage and ferocious spirit, and a degrading subserviency to royal resentments, real or supposed." †

ATTAINDERS PROHIBITED AS INCONSISTENT WITH CONSTITUTIONAL LIBERTY.

Bills of attainder struck at the root of all civil rights and political liberty. To declare single individuals, or

* 4 Bla. Com. 92.

† Lord Coke undertakes to justify the severity of this punishment by examples drawn from Scripture.

a large class of persons, criminals, in time of peace, merely upon the ground that they entertained certain opinions upon questions of church or state; to do this by act of Parliament, without a hearing, or after the death of the alleged offender; to involve the innocent with the guilty in indiscriminate punishment, — was an outrage upon the rights of the people not to be tolerated in our constitution as one of the powers of government.

BILLS OF ATTAINDER ABOLISHED.

The constitution provides expressly,* that "no bill of attainder, or *ex post facto* law, shall be passed by Congress; and that no State shall pass any bill of attainder, *ex post facto* law, or law impairing the obligation of contracts." † There is, therefore, no power in this country to pass any bill of attainder.

WHAT IS A BILL OF ATTAINDER?

Wherein does it differ from other statutes for the punishment of criminals?

A "bill of attainder," in the technical language of the law, is a statute by which the offender becomes "attainted," and is liable to punishment without having been convicted of any crime in the ordinary course of judicial proceedings.

If a person be expressly named in the bill, or comes within the terms thereof, he is liable to punishment. The legislature undertakes to pronounce upon the guilt of the accused party. He is entitled to no hearing, when living, and may be pronounced guilty when ab-

* Art. I. Sect. 9. † Art. I. Sect. 10.

sent from the country, or even long after his death. Lord Coke says that the reigning monarch of England, who was slain at Bosworth, is said to have been attainted by act of Parliament a few months after his death, notwithstanding the absurdity of deeming him at once in possession of a throne and a traitor.*

A question has been raised, whether any statute can be deemed a bill of attainder if it inflicts a degree of punishment less than that of death?

In technical law, statutes were called bills of attainder only when they inflicted the penalty of death or outlawry; while statutes which inflicted only forfeitures, fines, imprisonments, and similar punishments, were called bills of "pains and penalties." This distinction was practically observed in the legislation of England. No bill of attainder can probably be found which did not contain the marked feature of the death penalty, or the penalty of outlawry, which was considered as equivalent to a judgment of death. Judgment of outlawry on a capital crime, pronounced for absconding or fleeing from justice, was founded on that which was in law deemed a tacit confession of guilt.†

BILLS OF PAINS AND PENALTIES.

It has been said that within the sense of the constitution, bills of attainder include bills of pains and penalties; and this view seemed to derive support from a remark of a judge of the Supreme Court. "A bill of attainder may affect the life of an individual, or may confiscate his property, or both." ‡

* See Story on the Constitution, B. III. Sect. 678.

† Standf. Pl. Co. 44, 122, 182.

‡ *Fletcher* v. *Peck*, 6 Cranch, R.

It is true that a bill of attainder may affect the life of an individual; but if the individual attainted were dead before the passage of the act, as was the case with Richard III., the bill could not affect his life; or if a bill of attainder upon outlawry were passed against persons beyond seas, the life of the party would not be in fact affected, although the outlawry was equivalent in the eye of the law to civil death. There is nothing in this dictum inconsistent with the ancient and acknowledged distinction between bills of attainder and bills of pains and penalties; nothing which would authorize the enlargement of the technical meaning of the words; nothing which shows that Judge Marshall deemed that bills of attainder included bills of pains and penalties within the sense of the constitution. This dictum is quoted by Judge Story,* who supposed its meaning went beyond that which is now attributed to it. But he does not appear to sanction such a view of the law. This is the only authority to which he refers; and he introduces the proposed construction of this clause by language which is used by lawyers who have little confidence in the result which the authority indicates, viz., "it seems." No case has been decided by the Supreme Court of the United States which shows that "bills of attainder," within the sense of the constitution, include any other statutes than those which were technically so considered according to the law of England.

EX POST FACTO LAWS PROHIBITED. BILLS OF PAINS AND PENALTIES, AS WELL AS ATTAINDERS, UNCONSTITUTIONAL.

It does not seem important whether the one or the other construction be put upon the language of this

* Com. Const. III. Ch. 32, Sect. 3.

clause, nor whether bills of pains and penalties be or be not included within the prohibition; for Congress can pass no *ex post facto* law; and it was one of the invariable characteristics of bills of attainder, and of bills of pains and penalties, that they were passed for the punishment of supposed crimes which had been committed before the acts were passed.

The clause prohibiting Congress from passing any *ex post facto* law would doubtless have prevented their passing any bill of attainder; but this prohibition was inserted from greater caution, and to prevent the exercise of constructive powers against political offenders. No usurpation of authority in the worst days of English tyranny was more detested by the framers of our constitution than that which attempted to ride over the rights of Englishmen to gratify royal revenge against the friends of free government. Hence in that respect they shut down the gate upon this sovereign power of government. They forbade any punishment, under any form, for crime not against some standing law, which had been enacted before the time of its commission. They prevented Congress from passing any attainder laws, whereby the accused might be deprived of his life, or his estate, or both, without trial by jury, and by his political enemies; and whereby also his relatives would suffer equally with himself.

ATTAINDERS IN THE COLONIES AND STATES.

Bills in the nature of bills of attainder were familiar to our ancestors in most of the colonies and in the States which subsequently formed the Union. And several of these acts of attainder have been pronounced valid by the highest courts in these States. By the act of the State of New York, October 22, 1779, the real and personal property of persons adhering to the enemy was forfeited to the State ; and this act has been held valid,* and proceedings under acts of attainder were, as the court held, to be construed according to the rules in cases of attainder, and not by the ordinary course of judicial proceedings ; † and these laws applied to persons who were dead at the time of the proceedings. ‡

"Bills of attainder," says the learned judge, (in 2 Johnson's Cases,) "have always been construed in this respect with more latitude than ordinary judicial proceedings, for the purpose of giving them more certain effect, and that the intent of the legislature may prevail." "They are extraordinary acts of sovereignty, founded on public policy § and the peace of the community." "The attainted person," says Sir Matthew Hale, "is guilty of the execrable murder of the king." The act of New York, October 22, 1779, attainted, among others, Thomas Jones of the offence of adhering to the enemies of the State. This was a specific offence, and was not declared or understood to amount to treason, because many of the persons attainted had never owed allegiance to the State. ||

Bills of attainder were passed not only in New York, but in several other colonies and States, inflicting the penalties of attainder for other crimes than treason, actual or constructive. And the harsh operation of such laws, their injustice, and their liability to be abused

* *Sleight* v. *Kane*, 2 Johns. Cas. 236, decided in April, 1801.

† *Jackson* v. *Sands*, 2 Johns. 267.

‡ *Jackson* v. *Stokes*, 3 Johns. 15.

§ Foster, 83, 84.

|| *Jackson* v. *Catlin*, 2 Johns. R. 260.

in times of public excitement, were understood by those who laid the foundations of this government too well to permit them to disregard the dangers which they sought to avert, by depriving Congress, as well as the several States, of all power to enact such cruel statutes.

If bills of attainder had been passed only for the punishment of treason, in the sense of making war upon the government, or aiding the enemy, they would have been less odious and less dangerous; but the regiment of crimes which servile Parliaments had enrolled under the title of "treason," had become so formidable, and the brutality of the civil contests in England had been so shocking, that it was thought unsafe to trust any government with the arbitrary and irresponsible power of condemning by statute large classes of their opponents to death and destruction for that which only want of success had made a crime.

BILLS OF ATTAINDER, HOW RECOGNIZED.

The consequences of attainder to the estate of the party convicted will be more fully stated hereafter; but it is essential to observe that there are certain characteristics which distinguish bills of attainder from all other penal statutes.

1. They always inflict the penalty of death upon the offender, or of outlawry, which is equivalent to death.

2. They are always *ex post facto* laws, being passed after the crime was committed which they are to punish.

3. They never allow the guilt or innocence of the persons attainted to be ascertained by trial; but the guilt is attributed to them by act of Parliament.

4. They always inflicted certain penalties, among

which were corruption of blood and forfeiture of estate. The essence of attainder was in corruption of blood, and without the corruption of blood no person was by the English law attainted.

Unless a law of Congress shall contain these four characteristics — penalty of death, or outlawry, corruption of blood, and the legislative, not judicial condemnation — embodied in a law passed after the commission of the crime it seeks to punish, it is not a bill of attainder under the sense of the constitution.

CHAPTER V.

RIGHT OF CONGRESS TO DECLARE BY STATUTE THE PUNISHMENT OF TREASON, AND ITS CONSTITUTIONAL LIMITATIONS.

TREASON.

THE highest crime known to the law is *treason.* It is "the sum of all villanies;" its agents have been branded with infamy in all countries where fidelity and justice have respect. The name of one who betrays his friend becomes a byword and a reproach. How much deeper are the guilt and infamy of the criminal who betrays his country! No convict in our State prisons can have fallen so low as willingly to associate with a TRAITOR. There is no abyss of crime so dark, so horrible, as that to which the traitor has descended. He has left forever behind him conscience, honor, and hope.

ANCIENT ENGLISH DOCTRINE OF CONSTRUCTIVE TREASON.

Treason, as defined in the law of England, at the date of the constitution, embraced many misdemeanors which are not now held to be crimes. Offences of a political character, not accompanied with any intention to subvert the government; mere words of disrespect to the ruling sovereign; assaults upon the king's officers at certain times and places; striking one of the judges in court; and many other acts which did not partake of the nature of treason, were, in ancient times, declared treason by Parliament, or so construed by judges, as to constitute that crime. Indeed, there was nothing to prevent Parliament from proclaiming any act of a subject to be treason, thereby subjecting him to all its terrible penalties. The doctrine of *constructive treasons*, created by servile judges, who held their office during the pleasure of the king, was used by them in such a way as to enable the sovereign safely to wreak vengeance upon his victims under the guise of judicial condemnation. If the king sought to destroy a rival, the judges would pronounce him guilty of constructive treason; in other words, they would so construe the acts of the defendant as to make them treason. Thus the king could selfishly outrage every principle of law and justice, while avoiding responsibility. No man's life or property was safe. The wealthier the citizen, the greater was his apprehension that the king would seize and confiscate his estates. The danger lay in the fact that the nature and extent of the legal crime of treason was indeterminate, or was left to arbitrary determination. The power to *define* treason, to declare from time to time who should be deemed in law to be traitors, was in its nature an *arbitrary* power. No government having that power would fail to become oppressive in times of excitement, and especially in civil war. As early as the reign of Edward III., Parliament put an end to these judge-made-treasons by declaring and defining all the different acts which should be deemed treason; and, although subsequent statutes have added to or modified the law, yet treason has at all times since that reign been defined by statute.

POWER OF CONGRESS TO DEFINE AND PUNISH TREASON LIMITED.

It was with full knowledge of the history of judicial usurpation, of the tyranny of exasperated governments, and of the tendency of rival factions in republics to seek revenge on each other, that the convention which framed the constitution, having given no power to the judiciary, like that possessed by English judges, to make constructive crimes, introduced several provisions limiting the power of Congress to define and punish the political crime of treason, as well as other offences.

The various clauses in the constitution relating to this subject, in order to a clear exposition of their meaning, should be taken together as parts of our system.

ATTAINDER AND EX POST FACTO LAWS.

The first and most important limitation of the power of Congress is found in Art. I. Sect. 9: "No bill of attainder, or *ex post facto* law, shall be passed." By prohibiting bills of attainder, no subject could be made a criminal, or be deprived of life, liberty, or property, by mere *act of legislation*, without trial or conviction. The power to enact *ex post facto* laws having been withheld, Congress could not pass "a statute which would render an act punishable in a manner in which it was not punishable when it was committed." No man's life could be taken, his liberty abridged, nor his estate, nor any part of it, seized for an act which had not, previously to the commission thereof, been declared by some law as a crime, and the manner and extent of punishment prescribed.* Hence no law of Congress can make that deed a crime which was not so before the deed was done. Every man may know what are the

* See *Fletcher* v. *Peck*, 6 Cranch, 138.

laws to which he is amenable in time of peace by reading the statutes. There can be no retrospective criminal legislation by any State, or by the United States.

TREASON DEFINED BY STATUTE.

These points having been secured, the next step was to *define* the CRIME OF TREASON. Countless difficulties and dangers were avoided by selecting from the English statutes *one crime only*, which should be deemed to constitute that offence.

The constitution provides that, "Treason against the United States shall consist only in levying war against them, or in adhering to their enemies, giving them aid and comfort." * Hence many acts are not treasonable which were so considered according to the law of England, and of the colonies and States of this country. Each State still retains the power to define and punish treason against itself in its own way.

Nothing but *overt acts* are treasonable by the laws of the United States; and these overt acts must be overt acts of war.† These acts must be proved either by confession in open court, or by two witnesses to the same act. ‡ Our ancestors took care that no one should be convicted of this infamous crime, unless his guilt is made certain. So odious was the offence that even a senator or representative could be arrested on *suspicion* of it. § All civil officers were to be removed from office on impeachment and conviction thereof. || And a person charged with treason against a State, and fleeing from that State to another, was to be delivered

* Art. III. Sect. 3. † Ibid. ‡ Ibid.
§ Art. I. Sect. 6. || Art. II. Sect. 4.

up, on demand, to the State having jurisdiction.* The crime being defined, and the nature of the testimony to establish it being prescribed, and conviction being possible only in "open court," the constitution then provides, — that "Congress shall have power to declare the *punishment* of treason, but no attainder of treason shall work corruption of blood, or forfeiture, except during the life of the person attainted." †

CONGRESS HAVE UNLIMITED POWER TO DECLARE THE PUNISHMENT OF TREASON.

By this article, the constitution has in express terms given to Congress the power to declare the *punishment* of treason; and the nature and extent of the punishment which they may declare are not limited. Congress may impose the penalty of fine, or imprisonment, or outlawry, or banishment, or forfeiture, or death, or of death and forfeiture of property, personal and real. Congress might have added to all these punishments the more terrible penalty which followed, *as a consequence of attainder of treason,* under the law of England, had the constitution not limited the effect and operation of that species of attainder.

A COMMON ERROR.

Some writers have supposed that this article in the constitution, which qualifies the *effect* of an attainder of treason, was *a limitation* of the power of Congress to declare the *punishment* of treason. This is an error. A careful examination of the language used in the in-

* Constitution, Art. IV. Sect. 6.

† Art. III. Sect. 3.

strument itself, and of the history of the English law of attainder, will make it evident that the framers of the constitution, in drafting Sect. 3 of Art. III. did not design to restrain Congress from declaring against the traitor himself, his person or estate, such penalties as it might deem sufficient to atone for the highest of crimes.

Whenever a person had committed high treason in England, and had been duly indicted, tried, and convicted, and when final judgment of guilty, and sentence of death or outlawry, had been pronounced upon him, the immediate and inseparable consequence, by common law, of the sentence of death or outlawry of the offender for treason, and for certain other felonies, was *attainder.* Attainder means, in its original application, the staining or corruption of the blood of a criminal who was in the contemplation of law dead. He then became "*attinctus* — stained, blackened, attainted."

CONSEQUENCES OF ATTAINDER.

Certain legal results followed from *attainder,* among which are the following: The convict was no longer of any credit or reputation. He could not be a witness in any court. He was not capable of performing the legal functions of any other man; his power to sell or transfer his lands and personal estate ceased. By anticipation of his punishment he was already dead in law,* except when the fiction of the law would protect him from some liability to others which he had the power to discharge. It is true that the attainted felon could not be murdered with impunity,† but the law preserved

* 3 Inst. 213. † Foster, 73.

his physical existence only to vindicate its own majesty, and to inflict upon the offender an ignominious death.

CORRUPTION OF BLOOD.

Among the most important consequences of *attainder* of *felony*, were those *resulting from* "*corruption of blood*," which is the *essence of attainder*.* Blackstone says,† —

"Another immediate consequence of attainder is the corruption of blood, both upwards and downwards; so that an attainted person can neither inherit lands or other hereditaments from his ancestors, nor retain those he is already in possession of, nor transmit them by descent to any heir; but the same shall escheat to the lord of the fee, subject to the king's superior right of forfeiture; and the person attainted shall also obstruct all descents to his posterity whenever they are obliged to derive a title through him, to a remote ancestor."

The distinctions between escheat and forfeiture it is not necessary now to state,‡ because, whether the forfeiture enured to the benefit of the lord or of the king, the effect was the same upon the estate of the criminal.§ By this legal fiction of *corruption of blood*, the offender was deprived of all his estate, personal and real; his children or other heirs could not inherit any thing from him, nor through him from any of his ancestors. "If a father be seized in fee, and the son commits treason and is attainted, and then the father dies, then the lands shall escheat to the lord." ||

SAVAGE CRUELTY OF ENGLISH LAW.

By the English system of escheats to the lord and forfeitures to the king, the innocent relatives of the offender were punished, upon the theory that it was

* See Co. Litt. 391. † 4 Com. b. 388. ‡ See Co. Litt. 13.
§ Co. Litt. p. 391. Bla. Com. Vol. II. p. 254 || Co. Litt. p. 13.

the duty of every family to secure the loyalty of all its members to the sovereign; and upon failure to do so, the whole family should be plunged into lasting disgrace and poverty. A punishment which might continue for twenty generations, was indeed inhuman, and received, as it merited, the condemnation of liberal men in all countries; * but aristocratic influence in England had for centuries resisted the absolute and final abandonment of these odious penalties. The framers of the constitution have deprived Congress of the power of passing bills of attainder. They might have provided that no person convicted of treason should be held to be attainted, or be liable to suffer any of the common law penalties which resulted from attainder, but only such penalties as Congress should prescribe by statute. They have, however, not in terms, abolished attainders, but have modified their effect, by declaring that attainder shall not work corruption of blood.

FORFEITURES.

By the law of England, forfeiture of estates was also one of the necessary legal consequences of attainder of felony. Real estate was forfeited upon attainder, personal estate upon conviction before attainder. By these forfeitures all the property, rights, and claims, of every name and nature, went to the lord or the king. But forfeiture of lands related back to the time when the felony was committed, so as to avoid all subsequent sales and encumbrances, but forfeiture of goods took effect at the date of conviction, so that sales of personal property, prior to that time, were valid, unless col-

* See 4 Bla. Com. p. 388.

lusive.* The estates thus forfeited were not mere estates for life, but the whole interest of the felon, whatever it might be. Thus forfeiture of property was a consequence of attainder; attainder was a consequence of the sentence of death or outlawry; and these penal consequences of attainder were over and above, and in addition to, the penalties expressed in the terms of *the judgment* and *sentence of the court*.† The punishment, and in many instances the only punishment, to which the sentence of the court condemned the prisoner, was death or outlawry. The disabilities which resulted from that sentence were like the disabilities which in other cases result from the sentence of a criminal for infamous crimes. Disability to testify in courts, or to hold offices of trust and honor, sometimes follows, not as part of the punishment prescribed for the offence, but as a consequence of the condition to which the criminal has reduced himself.

There is a clear distinction between the punishment of treason by specific penalties and those consequential damages and injuries which follow by common law as the result or technical effect of a sentence of death or outlawry for treason, viz., attainder of treason, and corruption of blood and forfeiture of estates.‡ To set this subject in a clearer light, the learned reader will recollect that there were different kinds of attainder:

* See Stat. 13 Eliz. ch. 5; 2 B. & A. 258; 2 Hawkins's P. C. 454; 3 Ins. 232; 4 Bla. 387; Co. Litt. 391, b.

† See 2 Greenleaf's Cruise on Real Property, p. 145, and note; 2 Kent, 386; 1 Greenleaf's Cruise, p. 71, sect. 1, and note.

‡ There is a provision in the new constitution of Maryland, (1851,) that "no conviction shall work corruption of blood or forfeiture of estate." (Decl. of Rights, Art. 24.) The constitution of Ohio (1851) contains the same words in the 12th sect. of the Decl. of Rights. The constitutions of

1. *Attainders in a præmunire;* in which, "from the conviction, the defendant shall be out of the king's protection, his lands, tenements, goods, and chattels forfeited to the king, and his body remain in prison during the king's pleasure, or during life."* But the offences punishable under the statutes of præmunire were not felonies, for the latter are punishable only by common law, and not by statute.† 2. *Attainder by bill.* 3. *Attainders of* FELONY and treason; and the important distinction between attainders in treason and attainders in præmunire is this: that in the former the forfeitures are consequences of the judgment, in the latter they are part of the judgment and penalty. Blackstone‡ recognizes fully this distinction. "I here omit the particular forfeitures created by the statutes of præmunire and others, because I look upon them rather as a part of the judgment and penalty inflicted by the respective statutes, than as consequences of such judgment, as in treason and felony they are." Lord Coke expresses the

Kentucky, Delaware, and Pennsylvania declare that attainder of treason shall not work forfeiture beyond the lifetime of the offender. In Alabama, Connecticut, Indiana, Illinois, Maine, Missouri, New Jersey, Rhode Island, and Tennessee, all forfeitures for crime are abolished, either by statutes or constitutions.

"In New Hampshire, Massachusetts, Virginia, Georgia, Michigan, Mississippi, and Arkansas, there are statutes providing specifically for the punishment of treason and felonies; but no mention is made of corruption of blood or forfeiture of estate; and inasmuch as these offences are explicitly legislated upon, and a particular punishment provided in each case, it may be gravely doubted whether the additional common law punishment of forfeiture of estate ought not to be considered as repealed by implication." 1 Greenleaf's Cruise Dig. 196, note.

* 1 Inst. 129; 3 Bla. p. 118; and for the severity of the penalties, see 1 Hawk. P. C. 55.

† 4 Bla. 118.

‡ 4 Com. p. 386.

same opinion.* And statutes of præmunire and attainders of treason are both different in law from *bills of pains and penalties;* of which English history affords, among many other examples, that against the Bishop of Rochester; † in the latter the pains and penalties are all expressly declared by statute, and not left as consequences of judgment. That clause in the constitution which gives power to Congress to make laws for the punishment of treason, limits and qualifies the effect of attainder of treason, in case such attainder should be deemed by the courts as a legal consequence of such sentence as the statute requires the court to impose on traitors. This limitation applies, in terms, *only* to the effect of attainders of treason.

CHARACTERISTICS OF ATTAINDER OF TREASON.

There is no attainder of treason known to the law of England, unless, 1. The judgment of death or outlawry has been pronounced against the traitor. ‡ 2. Where the crime was a *felony,* and punishable according to common law; § and, 3. Where the attainder was a consequence of the judgment, and not part of the judgment and penalty. || Congress may pass a law condemning every traitor to death, and to the consequential punishment of "attainder;" but such attainder will not of itself operate to corrupt blood or forfeit estate, except during the life of the offender. But unless Congress pass a law expressly *attainting* the criminal of

* Co. Litt. 391, b.
† Stat. 9 Geo. I. ch. 17.
‡ 4 Bla. 387.
§ 4 Bla. 387.
|| Ib.; Co. Litt. 391, b.; 4 Bla. 386.

treason, there is not, under the laws of the United States, any "attainder." The criminal laws of the United States are all embraced in specific statutes, defining crimes and all their penalties. No consequential penalties of this character are known to this law. And if a person is convicted and sentenced to death for treason, there can be no corruption of blood, nor forfeiture of estate except by express terms of the statute. The leading principles of the constitution forbid the making of laws which should leave the penalty of crime to be determined by ancient or antiquated common law proceedings of English courts. Forfeiture of estate, by express terms of statute, may be in the nature of forfeiture by a bill of pains and penalties, or præmunire, but is not forfeiture by attainder; nor is it such forfeiture as is within the sense of the constitution, which limits the operation of attainders of treason. This distinction was well known to the framers of the constitution. They thought it best to guard against the danger of those constructive and consequential punishments, giving full power to Congress, in plain terms, to prescribe by statute what punishment they should select; but in case of resort to attainder of treason, as one of those punishments, that form of punishment should not be so construed as, *ex vi termini*, to corrupt blood nor forfeit estate except during the life of the person attainted.

TECHNICAL LANGUAGE TO BE CONSTRUED TECHNICALLY.

The language of the constitution is peculiar; it is technical; and it shows on the face of it an intention to limit the technical operation of attainders, not to limit the scope or extent of legislative penalties. If the authors of the constitution meant to say that Congress should pass no law punishing treason by attainder, or by its consequences, viz., forfeiture of estate, or corruption of blood, they would, in plain terms, have said so; and there would have been an end to the penalties of attainder, as there was an end to bills of attainder. Instead of saying, "Congress shall have power to declare the punishment of treason, but shall not impose the penalties of attainder upon the offender," they said, "Congress shall have power to declare the punishment of treason, but no attainder of treason shall work corruption of blood, or forfeiture, except during the life of the person attainted."

This phraseology has reference only to the technical effect of attainder. The "working of forfeitures" is a phrase used by lawyers to show the legal result or effect which arises from a certain state of facts. If a traitor is convicted, judgment of death is passed upon him; by that judgment he becomes attainted. Attainder works forfeitures and corruption of blood; forfeitures and corruption of blood are, in the ordinary course of common law, followed by certain results to his rights of property. But the constitution provides, if the traitor is attainted, that attainder shall not, *ex vi termini*, and of its own force, and without statute to that effect, "work" forfeiture or corruption of blood. The convict may still retain all those civil rights of which he has not been deprived by the strict terms of the statute which shall declare the punishment of treason.

The punishment of treason, by the statute of the United States of April 30, 1790, is death, and nothing more. Can any case be found, since the statute was enacted, in which a party convicted and adjudged guilty of treason and sentenced to death, has been held to be "attainted" of treason, so that the attainder has worked forfeiture of any of his estate, real or personal? Would not any lawyer feel astonishment if a court of the United States, having sentenced a traitor to death under the law of 1790, should announce as a further penalty the forfeiture of the real and personal estate of the offender, "worked" by the attainder of felony, notwithstanding no such penalty is mentioned in that statute?

If Congress should pass an act punishing a traitor by a fine of five dollars, and imprisonment for five years, who would not feel amazed to learn that by the English doctrine of forfeitures worked by attainders, by operation of law, the criminal might be stripped of property worth thousands of dollars, over and above the penalty prescribed by statute?

TRUE MEANING OF ART. III. SECT. III. CL. II.

The constitution means that if traitors shall be attainted, unlimited forfeitures and corruption of blood shall not be worked by attainders. It means to leave untrammelled the power of Congress to cause traitors to be attainted or otherwise; but if attainted Congress must provide by statute for the attainder; and the constitution settles how far that attainder shall operate constitutionally; and when the legislature has awarded one punishment for treason, the law shall not evoke the doctrine of forfeitures worked by attainder, and thus, by technical implication, add punishments not specifically set down in the penal statute itself; or if this implication exist, the results of the technical effect of attainder shall not be corruption of blood, or forfeiture, except during the life of the offender. The third article does not limit the power of Congress to punish, but it limits the technical consequences of a special kind of punishment, which may or may not be adopted in the statutes.

From the foregoing remarks it is obvious that no person is attainted of treason, in the technical sense, who is convicted under the United States act of 1790. There can be no attainder of treason, within the meaning of the constitution, unless there be, first, a judgment of death, or outlawry; second, a penalty of attainder by express terms of the statute. A mere conviction of treason and sentence of death, or outlawry, and forfeitures of real and personal estate, do not constitute an attainder in form, in substance, nor in effect, when made under any of the present statutes of the United States.

IF CONGRESS MAY IMPOSE FINES, WHY NOT FORFEITURES?

No one doubts the power of Congress to make treason punishable with death, or by fines to any amount whatever. Nor would any reasonable person deem any fine too large to atone for the crime of involving one's own country in civil war. If the constitution placed in Congress the power to take life, and to take property of the offender in one form, why should it deny the power to take property in any other form? If the framers of the constitution were willing that a traitor should forfeit his life, how could they have intended to shelter his property? Was property, in their opinion, more sacred than life? Would all the property of rebels forfeited to the treasury of the country repair the injury of civil war?

FORFEITURES NOT LIMITED TO LIFE ESTATES.

Could the lawyers who drafted the constitution have intended to limit the pecuniary punishment of forfeiture to a life interest in personal estate, when every lawyer in the convention must have known than at common law there was no such thing as a life estate in personal property? Knowing this, did they mean to protect traitors, under all circumstances, in the enjoyment of personal property? If so, why did they not say so? If they meant to prevent Congress from passing any law that should deprive traitors of more than a life estate in real estate, the result would be, that the criminal would lose only the enjoyment of his lands for a few days or weeks, from the date of the judgment to the date of his execution, and then his lands would go to his heirs. Thus it is evident, that if the constitution cuts off the power of Congress to punish treason, and limits it to such forfeitures as are the consequence of attainder, and then cuts off from attainder its penal consequences of corruption of blood and forfeiture of estate, except during the life of the offender, then the framers of that instrument have effectually protected the personal and real estate of traitors, and have taken more care to secure them from the consequences of their crime than any other class of citizens. If so, they have authorized far more severity against many other felons than against them. If such were the purpose of the authors of the constitution, they would have taken direct and plain language to say what they meant. They would have said, "Congress may punish treason, but shall not deprive traitors of real or personal property, except for the time which may elapse between sentence of death and execution." Instead of such a provision, they gave full power to punish treason, including fines, absolute forfeitures, death, and attainder, only limiting the technical effect of the last-mentioned penalty, if that form of punishment should be adopted; and Congress has the power, under the constitution, to declare as the penalty for treason the forfeiture of all the real and personal estate of the offender, and is not limited, as has been supposed by some, to a forfeiture of real estate for life only.

CHAPTER VI.

STATUTES AGAINST TREASON. WHAT THEY ARE, AND HOW THEY ARE TO BE ADMINISTERED.

THE United States statute of April 30th, 1790, provides that,—

"If any person or persons, owing allegiance to the United States of America, shall levy war against them, or shall adhere to their enemies, giving them aid and comfort, within the United States or elsewhere, and shall be thereof convicted, on confession in open court, or on the testimony of two witnesses to the same overt act of the treason whereof he or they shall stand indicted, such person or persons shall be adjudged *guilty* of *treason* against the United States, and *shall suffer death.*"

Concealment of knowledge of treason (misprision of treason) is, by the same act, punished by fine not exceeding one thousand dollars, and imprisonment not exceeding seven years. By the statute of January 30th, 1799, corresponding with foreign governments, or with any officer or agent thereof, with intent to influence their controversies with the United States, or to defeat the measures of this government, is declared to be a high misdemeanor, though not called treason, and is punishable by fine not exceeding five thousand dollars, and imprisonment during a term not less than six months, nor exceeding three years. So the law has stood during this century, until the breaking out of the present rebellion.

The chief provisions of the law passed at the last session of Congress, and approved July 17th, 1862, are these:—

Section 1. Persons committing treason shall suffer one of two punishments: 1. Either death, and freedom to his slaves; or, 2. Imprisonment not less than five years, fine not less than ten thousand dollars, and freedom of slaves; the fine to be collected out of any personal or real estate except slaves.

Sect. 2. Inciting rebellion, or engaging in it, or aiding those who do so, is punishable by imprisonment not more than ten years, fine not more than ten thousand dollars, and liberation of slaves.

Sect. 3 disqualifies convicts, under the preceding sections, from holding office under the United States.

Sect. 4 provides that former laws against treason shall not be suspended as against any traitor, unless he shall have been convicted under this act.

Sect. 5 makes it the duty of the President to cause the seizure of all the property, real and personal, of several classes of persons, and to apply the same to the support of the army, namely: 1. Rebel army and navy officers; 2. Government officers of Confederate States in their national capacity; 3. Confederate State officers; 4. United States officers turned traitor officers; 5. Any one holding any office or agency, national, state, or municipal, under the rebel government, *provided* persons enumerated in classes 3, 4, and 5 have accepted office since secession of the State, or have taken oath of allegiance to support the Confederate States; 6. Persons who, owning property in loyal States, in the territories, or in the District of Columbia, shall hereafter assist, aid, or comfort such rebellion. All transfers of property so owned shall be null, and suits for it by such persons shall be barred by proving that they are within the terms of this act.

Sect. 6. Any persons within the United States, not above named, who are engaged in armed rebellion, or aiding and abetting it, who shall not, within sixty days after proclamation by the President, "cease to aid, countenance, and abet said rebellion," shall be liable to have all their property, personal and real, seized by the President, whose duty it shall be to seize and use it, or the proceeds thereof. All transfers of such property, made more than sixty days after the proclamation, are declared null.

Sect. 7. To secure the condemnation and sale of seized property, so as to make it available, proceedings *in rem* shall be instituted in the name of the United States, in any District Court thereof, or in any territorial court, or in the United States District Court for the District of Columbia, within which district or territory the property, or any part of it, may be found, or into which, if movable, it may first be brought. Proceedings are to conform to those in admiralty or revenue cases. Condemnation shall be as of enemy's property, and it shall belong to the United States; the proceeds thereof to be paid into the treasury.

Sect. 8. Proper powers are given to the courts to carry the above proceedings into effect, and to establish legal forms and processes and modes of transferring condemned property.

Sect. 9. Slaves of rebels, or of those aiding them, escaping and taking refuge within the lines of our army; slaves captured from them; slaves deserted by them, and coming under the control of the United States government; slaves found in places occupied by rebel forces, and afterwards occupied by the United States army, shall be deemed captives of war, and shall be forever *free*.

Sect. 10. No fugitive slave shall be returned to a

person claiming him, nor restrained of his liberty, except for crime, or offence against law, unless the claimant swears that the person claiming the slave is his lawful owner, has not joined the rebellion, nor given aid to it. No officer or soldier of the United States shall surrender fugitive slaves.

Sect. 11. The President may employ, organize, and use as many persons of African descent as he pleases to suppress the rebellion, and use them as he judges for the public welfare.

Sect. 12. The President may make provisions for colonizing such persons as may choose to emigrate, after they shall have been freed by this act.

Sect. 13. The President is authorized by proclamation to pardon any persons engaged in the rebellion, on such terms as he deems expedient.

Sect. 14. Courts of the United States have full powers to institute proceedings, make orders, &c., to carry the foregoing measures into effect.

A resolution, explanatory of the above act, declares that the statute punishes no act done prior to its passage; and no judge or member of a State legislature, who has not taken the oath of allegiance to support the constitution of the Confederate States; nor shall any punishment or proceedings be so construed as to "work forfeiture of the real estate of the offender beyond his natural life."

The President's proclamation, in accordance with the above act, was issued July 25th, 1862. Thus all persons engaged in the rebellion, who come within the provisions of the sixth section, will be liable to the penalties after sixty days from July 25th. This is one of the most important penal acts ever passed by the Congress of the United States.

THE CONFISCATION ACT OF 1862 IS NOT A BILL OF ATTAINDER, NOR AN EX POST FACTO LAW.

This act is not a *bill of attainder*, because it does not punish the offender in any instance with corruption of blood, and it does not declare him, *by act of legislature*, guilty of treason, inasmuch as the offender's guilt must be duly proved and established by judicial proceedings before he can be sentenced. It is not an *ex post facto* law, as it declares no act committed prior to the time when the law goes into operation to be a crime, or to be punishable as such. It provides for no *attainder* of treason, and therefore for none of the penal consequences which might otherwise have followed from such attainder.

The resolution, which is to be taken as part of the act, or as explanatory of it, expressly provides that no punishment or proceedings under said act shall be so construed as to work a forfeiture of the real estate of the offender beyond his natural life. Thus, to prevent our courts from construing the sentence of death, under Sect. 1, as involving an attainder of treason, and its consequences, Congress has, in express terms, provided that no punishment or proceeding shall be so construed as to work forfeiture, as above stated. Thus this statute limits the constructive penalties which result from forfeitures worked by attainders, and perhaps may be so construed as to confine the punishments to those, and those only, which are prescribed in the plain terms of the statute. And this limitation is in accordance with the constitution, as understood by the President, although the forfeiture of rebels' real estate might have been made absolute and unlimited, without exceeding the constitutional power of Congress to punish treason.

CHAPTER VII.

THE RIGHT OF CONGRESS TO DECLARE THE PUNISHMENT OF CRIMES AGAINST THE UNITED STATES OTHER THAN TREASON.

THE NEW CRIMES OF REBELLION REQUIRE NEW PENAL LAWS.

Several crimes may be committed not defined as treason in the constitution, but not less dangerous to the public welfare. The prevention or punishment of such offences is essential to the safety of every form of government; and the power of Congress to impose penalties in such cases cannot be reasonably questioned. The rights guaranteed in express terms to private citizens cannot be maintained, nor be made secure, without such penal legislation; and, accordingly, Congress has, from time to time, passed laws for this purpose. The present rebellion has given birth to a host of crimes which were not previously punishable by any law. Among these crimes are the following: Accepting or holding civil offices under the Confederate government; violating the oath of allegiance to the United States; taking an oath of allegiance to the Confederate States; manufacturing, passing, or circulating a new and illegal currency; acknowledging and obeying the authority of a seceded State, or of the Confederate States; neglecting or refusing to return to allegiance and to lay down arms after due warning; attempting to negotiate treaties with foreign powers to intervene in our affairs; granting or taking letters of marque; conspiracy against the lawful government; holding public meetings to incite the people to the commission of treason; plotting treason; framing and passing ordinances of secession; organizing and forming new governments within any of the States, with the intent that they shall become independent of the United States, and hostile thereto; the making of treaties between the several States; refusal to take the oath of allegiance to the United States, when tendered by proper authority; resistance to civil process, or to civil officers of the United States, when such resistance is not so general as to constitute war. Each of these and many other public wrongs may be so committed as to avoid the penalty of treason, because they may not be overt acts of levying war, or of aiding and comforting the enemy, which the offender must have committed before he can have rendered himself liable to be punished for treason as defined in the constitution. These and other similar offences are perpetrated for the purpose of overthrowing government. Civil war must inevitably result from them. They might be deemed less heinous than open rebellion, if it were not certain that they are the fountain from which the streams of treason and civil war must flow, sweeping the innocent and the guilty with resistless tide onward to inevitable destruction.

ALL ATTEMPTS TO OVERTURN GOVERNMENT SHOULD BE PUNISHED.

Of the many atrocious misdeeds which are preliminary to or contemporaneous with treason, each and all may be and should be punishable by law. It is by no means desirable that the punishment of all of them should be by *death*, but rather by that penalty, which, depriving the criminal of the means of doing harm, will disgrace him in the community he has dishonored. Imprisonment, fines, forfeitures, confiscation, are the proper punishments for such hardened criminals, because imprisonment is a personal punishment, and fines, forfeitures, &c., merely transfer the property of the offender to the public, as a partial indemnity for the wrong he has committed.

When the terrible consequences of the crimes which foment civil war are considered, no penalty would seem too severe to expiate them. But it has been erroneously suggested that, as the levying of war — treason —itself is not punishable by depriving traitors of more than a life estate in their real estate, even though they are condemned to death, it could not have been the intention of the framers of the constitution to punish any of the crimes which may originate a civil war, by penalty equally severe with that to which they limited Congress, in punishing treason itself. A lower offence, it is said, should not be punished with more severity than a higher one. This objection would be more plausible if the power to punish treason were in fact limited. But, as has been shown in a previous chapter, such is not the fact.*

ACT OF 1862, SECTION VI., DOES NOT PURPORT TO PUNISH TREASON.

If the penalty of death be not inflicted on the guilty, and if he be not accused of treason, no question as to the validity of the statute could arise under this clause of the constitution limiting the effect of attainders of treason. No objection could be urged against its

* See Chap. V. page 93.

validity on the ground of its forfeiting or confiscating all the property of the offender, or of its depriving him of liberty by imprisonment, or of its exiling him from the country.

Section 6 of the act of 1862 does not impose the penalty of *death*, but it provides that if rebels in arms shall not, within sixty days after proclamation by the President, cease to aid and abet the rebellion, and return to their allegiance, they shall be liable to have all their property seized and used for the benefit of the country.

Suppose the rebels in arms refuse to obey the proclamation, and neglect or refuse to return to their allegiance; the mere non-performance of the requisition of this act is, *not levying war*, or aiding and comforting the enemy, technically considered, and so not treason — although, if they go on to perform overt acts in aid of the rebels, *those acts* will be treasonable. Will it be denied that the rebels in arms ought to be required by law to return to their allegiance and cease rebellion? If their refusal to do so is not technically treason, ought they not to be liable to punishment for violating the law? Is any degree of pecuniary loss too severe for those who will continue at war with their country after warning and proclamation, if their lives are not forfeited?

LEGAL CONSTRUCTION OF THE ACT OF 1862.

What will be the construction put upon section 6th of the act of 1862, when taken in connection with the joint resolution which accompanied it, is not so certain as it should be. The language of the last clause in that resolution is, "Nor shall any punishment or proceedings, under said act, be so construed as to work a 'forfeiture' of the real estate of the offender beyond his natural life." There is no forfeiture in express terms provided for in any part of the act. The punishment of treason, in the first section, is either death and freedom of slaves, or imprisonment, fine, and freedom of slaves. The judgment of death for treason is the only one which could, even by the common law, have been so construed as to "work any forfeiture." It may have been the intention of Congress to limit the constructive effect of such a judgment. But the words of the resolution are peculiar; they declare that no "proceedings" under said act shall be so construed as to work a forfeiture, &c. Then the question will arise whether the "proceedings" (authorized by section 6, in which the President has the power and duty to seize and use all the property of rebels in arms who refuse, after warning, to return to their allegiance) are such that a sale of such real estate, under the provisions of sections 7 and 8, can convey any thing more than an estate for the life of the offender? But the crime punished by section 6 is not the *crime of treason;* and whether there be or be not a limitation to the power of the legislature to punish that crime, there is no limit to its power to punish the crime described in this section.

Forfeiture and confiscation of real and personal estates for crimes, when there was and could have been no treason, were common and familiar penal statutes in several States or colonies when the constitution was framed. Many of the old tories, in the time of the revolution, were *banished,* and their real estate confiscated, without having been tried for or accused of treason, or having incurred any forfeiture by the laws against treason. Such was the case in South Carolina in 1776.* In that State, one set of laws was in force against treason, the punishment of which was forfeiture *worked by attainder.* Another set of laws were confiscation acts against tory *refugees* who had committed no treason. These distinctions were familiar to those who formed the constitution, and they used language relating to these subjects with technical precision.

THE SEVERITY OF DIFFERENT PUNISHMENTS COMPARED.

Forfeiture and confiscation are, in the eye of the law, less severe punishments than death: they are in effect fines, to the extent to which the criminal is capable of paying them. It would not seem to be too severe a punishment upon a person who seeks, with arms in his hands, to destroy your life, to steal or carry away your property, to subvert your government, that he should be deprived of his property by confiscation or fine to any amount he could pay. Therefore, as the provisions of section 6, which would authorize the seizure and appropriation of rebel real estate to public use, are not within the prohibitions of Art. III. Sect. 3 of the constitution, it is much to be regretted that the joint resolution of Congress should have been so worded as to throw a doubt upon the construction of that part of the statute, if not to paralyze its effect upon the only class of rebel property which they cannot put out of the reach of government, viz., their real estate.

* See *Willis* v. *Martin,* 2 Bay 20. See also *Hinzleman* v. *Clarke and Al.,* Coxe N. J., 1795.

THE SIXTH SECTION OF THE CONFISCATION ACT OF 1862 IS NOT WITHIN THE PROHIBITION OF THE CONSTITUTION, ARTICLE III. SECTION III.

Congress cannot, by giving a new name to acts of treason, transcend the constitutional limits in declaring its punishment. Nor can legislation change the true character of crimes. Hence some have supposed that Congress has no right to punish the most flagrant and outrageous acts of civil war by penalties more severe than those prescribed, as they say, for treason. Since a subject must have performed some overt act, which may be construed by courts into the "levying of war," or "aiding the enemy," before he can be convicted of treason, it has been supposed that to involve a great nation in the horrors of civil war can be nothing more, and nothing else, than treason. This is a mistake. The constitution does not define the meaning of the phrase "levying war." Is it confined to the true, and genuine signification of the words, namely, "that to levy war is to raise or begin war; to take arms for attack;" or must it be extended to include the carrying on or waging war, after it has been commenced?* The crime committed by a few individuals by merely *levying* war, or beginning without prosecuting or continuing armed resistance to government, although it is treason, may be immeasurably less than that of carrying on a colossal rebellion, involving millions in a fratricidal contest. Though treason is the highest *political* crime known to the codes of law, yet wide-spread and savage rebellion

* To *levy war* is to *raise* or *begin war;* to take arms for attack; to attack.—Webster's Quarto Dict.

To *levy* is, 1. To *raise*, as a siege. 2. To raise or collect; to gather. 3. To *raise*, applied to *war*.—Worcester's Quarto Dict.

is a still higher crime against society; for it embraces a cluster of atrocious wrongs, of which the attack upon government — treason — is but one. Although there can be no treason unless the culprit levies war, or aids the enemy, yet it by no means follows that all acts of carrying on a war once levied are *only* acts of treason. Treason is the threshold of war; the traitor passes over it to new and deeper guilt. He ought to suffer punishment proportioned to his crimes.

It must also be remembered, that the constitution does not indicate that fines, forfeitures, confiscations, outlawry, or imprisonment are "severer penalties than death." The law has never so treated them. Nor is there any limit to the power of Congress to punish traitors, as has been shown in a previous chapter.* Who will contend that the crime of treason is in morals more wicked, in its tendencies more dangerous, or in its results more deadly than the conspiracy by which it was plotted and originated? Yet suppose the conspirator is artful enough not to commit any overt act in presence of two witnesses; he cannot be convicted of treason, though he may have been far more guilty than many thoughtless persons who have been put forward to execute the "overt acts," and have thereby become punishable as traitors. Suppose a person commit homicide; he may be accused of assault and battery, or assault with intent to kill, or justifiable homicide, or manslaughter, or murder in either degree. Suppose the constitution limited the punishment of wilful murder to the death of the criminal and forfeiture of his real and personal estate for life; would any person contend that neither of the other above-mentioned crimes could

* See Chap. V. p. 93.

be punished, unless the criminal were convicted of wilful murder? If he had committed murder, he must have committed all the crimes involved in murder. He must have made an assault with intent to kill; and he must have committed unjustifiable homicide, or manslaughter. If the government should, out of leniency, prosecute and convict him of manslaughter, and impose upon him a penalty of fine, or confiscation of his real and personal estate, instead of sentence of death, would any one say that the penalty imposed was severer than death? or that murder was legislated into any other crime? or that any other crime was legislated into murder? Many crimes of different grades may coexist, and culminate in one offence. It is no sign of undue severity to prosecute the offender for one less than the highest. The same course of crime may violate many of the duties the loyal citizen owes to his country. To pass laws declaring the penalty for each and all of these crimes does not transcend the true scope of the criminal legislation of Congress, where an offender has brought upon his country the horrors of civil war by destroying the lives of those who have given him no cause of offence, by violating the rights of the living and the dead, by heaping upon his guilty act the criminality of a thousand assassins and murderers, and by striking at the root of the peace and happiness of a great nation; it does not seem unduly severe to take from him his property and his life. The constitution does not protect him from the penalty of death; and it cannot be so interpreted as to protect him against confiscation of his real estate.

TREASON AND CONFISCATION LAWS IN 1862. THEIR PRACTICAL OPERATION.

To understand the practical operation of the statutes now in force for the punishment of treason and rebellion, and for the seizure and confiscation of rebel property, it is necessary to observe the effect of other statutes which regulate the modes of procedure in the United States courts. Section 1 of the act of 1862, which, as well as the act of 1790, prescribes the punishment of death for treason; section 2, which imposes fines and penalties; section 3, which adds disqualification for office; and, in fact, all the penal sections of this statute, — entitle the accused to a judicial trial. Before he can be made liable to suffer any penalty, he must have been "pronounced guilty of the offence charged," and he must have suffered "judgment and sentence on conviction." The accused cannot by law be subjected to a trial unless he has previously been indicted by a grand jury. He cannot be adjudged guilty unless upon a verdict of a petty jury, impanelled according to law, and by courts having jurisdiction of the person and of the alleged offence. A brief examination of the statutes regulating such proceedings will show that treason and confiscation laws will not be likely to prove effectual, unless they shall be amended, or unless other statutes shall be so modified as to adapt them to the present condition of the country.

LEGAL RIGHTS OF PERSONS ACCUSED OF TREASON.

All judicial convictions must be in accordance with the laws establishing the judiciary and regulating its proceedings. Whenever a person accused of crime is held by the government, not as a belligerent or prisoner of war, but merely as a citizen of the United States, then he is amenable to, and must be tried under and by virtue of, standing laws; and all rights guaranteed to other citizens in his condition must be conceded to him.

WILL SECESSIONISTS INDICT AND CONVICT EACH OTHER?

No person can lawfully be compelled to appear and answer to a charge for committing capital or otherwise infamous crimes, except those arising in the army and navy, when in actual service, in time of war or public danger, until he has been indicted by a grand jury.* That grand jury is summoned by the marshal from persons in the district where the crime was committed.

By the statute of September 24, 1789, section 29, "in all cases punishable with death, the trial shall be had in the county where the offence was committed; or where that cannot be done without great inconvenience, twelve petit jurors at least shall be summoned from thence." It has indeed been decided that the judges are not obliged to try these cases in the county where the crime was committed, but they are bound to try them within the district in which they were perpetrated.†

HOW THE JURIES ARE SELECTED, AND THEIR POWERS.

The juries are to be designated by lot, or according to the mode of forming juries practised in 1789, so far as practicable: the qualifications of jurors must be the same as those required by the laws of the State where

* Constitutional Amendment V.

† *United States* v. *Wilson*, Baldw. 117; *United States* v. *Cornell*, 2 Mass. 95–98; *United States* v. *The Insurgents*, 3 Dall. 518.

the trial is held, in order to qualify them to serve in the highest court of that State; and jurors shall be returned from such parts of the district, from time to time, as the court shall direct, so as to be most favorable to an impartial trial. And if so many jurors are challenged as to prevent the formation of a full jury, for want of numbers, the panel shall be completed from the bystanders.

STATE RIGHTS AND SECESSION DOCTRINES IN THE JURY ROOM.

The jury are by law judges of the law and the fact, according to the opinion of many eminent lawyers and judges. Whether this be so or not, their verdict, being upon the law and the fact, in a criminal case, they become in effect judges of law and fact. Suppose that the judge presiding at the trial is honest and loyal, and that the jury is composed of men who believe that loyalty to the State is paramount to loyalty to the United States; or that the States had, and have, a lawful right to secede from the Union. Whatever the opinions of the judge presiding in the United States court might be on these questions, he would have no power to root out from the jury their honest belief, that obedience to the laws of their own seceding State is not, and cannot be, treason. The first step towards securing a verdict would be to destroy the belief of the jury in these doctrines of State rights, paramount State sovereignty, and the right of secession. To decide the issue, according to the conscientious judgment of the jurymen upon the facts and the law, would require them to find a verdict against the United States.

SYMPATHY.

But this is not the only difficulty in the operation of this statute. The grand jurors and the petit jury are to be drawn from those who are neighbors, and possibly friends, of the traitors. The accused has the further advantage of knowing, before the time of trial, the names of all the jurors, and of all the witnesses to be produced against him; he has the benefit of counsel, and the process of the United States to compel the attendance of witnesses in his behalf.* How improbable is it that any jury of twelve men will be found to take away the lives or estates of their associates, when some of the jurymen themselves, or their friends and relatives or debtors, are involved in the same offence! Could any judge reasonably expect a jury of horse thieves to convict one of their own number, when either of the jurymen might be the next man required to take his turn in the criminal box? Under the present state of the law, it is not probable that there will ever be a conviction, even if laws against treason, and those which confiscate property, were not unpopular and odious in a community against whom they are enacted. When an association of traitors and conspirators can be found to convict each other, then these statutes will punish treason, but not sooner.

LAWS ARE MOST EFFECTIVE WHICH REQUIRE NO REBEL TO ADMINISTER THEM.

Those sections of the act of 1862, empowering government to seize rebel property, real, personal, and mixed, and to apply it to the use of the army, to secure the condemnation and sale of seized property, so as to

* Statute of April 30, 1790, Sect. 29.

make it available, and to authorize proceedings *in rem*, conformably to proceedings in admiralty or revenue cases, are of a different and far more effective character. Those clauses in the act which allow of the employment in the service of the United States of colored persons, so far as they may be serviceable, and the freeing of the slaves of rebels, whether captured, seized, fugitive, abandoned, or found within the lines of the army, may be of practical efficacy, because these measures do not require the aid of any secession jury to carry them into effect.

STATUTES OF LIMITATION WILL PROTECT TRAITORS.

The statutes limiting the time during which rebels and traitors shall be liable to indictment ought also to be considered. By the act of 1790, no person can be punished unless indicted for treason within three years after the treason was committed, if punishable capitally; nor unless indicted within two years from the time of committing any offence punishable with fine or forfeiture. Thus, by the provisions of these laws, if the war should last two years, or if it should require two or three years after the war shall have been ended to reëstablish regular proceedings in courts, all the criminals in the seceded States will escape by the operation of the statutes of limitations. It is true, that if traitors flee from justice these limitations will not protect them; but this exception will apply to few individuals, and those who flee will not be likely to be caught. Unless these statutes are modified, those who have caused and maintained the rebellion will escape from punishment.

CHAPTER VIII.

INTERFERENCE OF GOVERNMENT WITH THE DOMESTIC AFFAIRS OF THE STATES.

PARTY PLATFORMS CANNOT ALTER THE CONSTITUTION.

POLITICAL parties, in times of peace, have often declared that they do not intend to interfere with slavery in the States. President Buchanan denied that government had any power to coerce the seceded States into submission to the laws of the country. When President Lincoln called into service the army and navy, he announced that it was not his purpose to interfere with the rights of loyal citizens, nor with their domestic affairs. Those who have involved this country in bloody war, all sympathizers in their treason, and others who oppose the present administration, unite in denying the right of the President or of Congress to interfere with slavery, even if such interference is the only means by which the Union can be saved from destruction. No constitututional power can be obliterated by any denial or abandonment thereof, by individuals, by political parties, or by Congress.

The war power of the President to emancipate enemy's slaves has been the subject of a preceding chapter. Congress having power to pass all laws "necessary and proper to provide for the public welfare and common defence of the country," as has been explained in Chapters I. and II., it is the sole judge of what legislation the public welfare and defence require;

it may enact laws abolishing slavery, whenever slavery, ceasing to be *merely* a private and domestic relation, becomes a matter of *national* concern, and the public welfare and defence cannot be provided for and secured without interfering with slaves. Laws passed for that purpose, in good faith, against belligerent subjects, not being within any express prohibition of the constitution, cannot lawfully be declared void by any department of government. Reasons and authority for these propositions have been stated in previous chapters.

DOMESTIC INSTITUTIONS.

Among the errors relating to slavery which have found their way into the public mind,— errors traceable directly to a class of politicians who are now in open rebellion,— the most important is, that *Congress has no right to interfere in any way with slavery.* Their assumption is, that the States in which slaves are held are alone competent to pass any law relating to an institution which belongs exclusively to the domestic affairs of the States, and in which Congress has no right to interfere in any way whatever.

From a preceding chapter, (see page 17,) it will be seen, that if slaves are *property*, property can be interfered with under the constitution; if slavery is a *domestic* institution, as *Mormonism* or *apprenticeship* is, each of them can lawfully be interfered with and annulled. But slavery has a double aspect. So long as it remains in truth "*domestic*," that is to say, according to Webster's Dictionary, "*pertaining to house or home*," so long government cannot be affected by it, and have no ground for interfering with it; when, on the contrary, it no longer pertains only to house and home, but enters into vital questions of war, aid and comfort to public enemies, or any of the national interests involved in a gigantic rebellion; when slavery, rising above its comparative insignificance as a household affair, becomes a vast, an overwhelming power, which is used by traitors to overthrow the government, and may be used by government to overthrow traitors, it then ceases to be *merely* domestic; it becomes a *belligerent power*, acting against the "public welfare and common defence." No institution continues to be simply "domestic" after it has become the effective means of aiding and supporting a public enemy.

When an "institution" compels three millions of subjects to become belligerent traitors, because they are slaves of disloyal masters, slavery becomes an affair which is of the utmost public and national concern. But the constitution *not only empowers*, but, under certain contingencies, *requires* slavery in the States to be interfered with. No one who will refer to the sections of that instrument here cited, will probably venture to deny the power of Congress, in one mode or another, to *interfere* for or against the institution of slavery.

CONGRESS MAY PASS LAWS INTERFERING FOR THE PRESERVATION AND PROTECTION OF SLAVERY IN THE STATES.

Art. IV. Sect. 2, required that fugitive slaves should be *delivered up*, and the fugitive slave laws were passed to carry this clause into effect.

Art. I. Sect. 9, required that the foreign slave trade should not be interfered with prior to 1808, but allowed an importation tax to be levied on each slave, not exceeding ten dollars per head.

Art. V. provided that no amendment of the constitution should be made, prior to 1808, affecting the preceding clause.

Art. I. Sect. 2 provides that three fifths of all slaves shall be included in representative numbers.

CONGRESS MAY INTERFERE AGAINST SLAVERY IN THE STATES.

Art. I. Sect. 8. Congress has power to regulate commerce with foreign nations, and among the several States, and with the Indian tribes. Under this clause Congress can in effect prohibit the *inter-state slave trade,* and so pass laws diminishing or destroying the value of slaves in the border States, and practically *abolish slavery* in those States.

CONGRESS MAY INTERFERE WITH SLAVERY BY CALLING UPON THE SLAVES, AS SUBJECTS, TO ENTER MILITARY SERVICE.

Art. I. Sect. 8. Congress has the power to declare war and make rules for the government of land and naval forces, and under this power to decide who shall *constitute the militia of the United States,* and to enrol and compel into the service of the United States *all the slaves,* as well as their masters, and thus to interfere with slavery in the States.

CONGRESS MAY INTERFERE WITH SLAVERY IN THE STATES BY CUTTING OFF THE SUPPLY OF SLAVES TO SUCH STATES.

The law now prohibiting the importation of slaves, and making slave trading piracy, is an interference with slavery, by preventing their introduction into the slave States. So also is the treaty with England to suppress the slave trade, and to keep an armed naval force on the coast of Africa.

In case of servile insurrection against the laws and

authority of the United States, the government *are bound to interfere with slavery*, as much as in an insurrection of their masters, which may also require a similar interference. The President, with the advice and consent of the Senate, has the power to make treaties; and, under the treaty-making power, slavery can be and has been interfered with. In the last war with Great Britain, a treaty was made to evacuate all the forts and places in the United States without carrying away any of the slaves who had gone over to them in the States. Congress then interfered to *sustain* the institution of slavery, for it was only by *sustaining* slavery that this government could claim indemnity for slaves as *property*. The *treaty-making power* may abolish slavery in the whole country, as, by Art. VI., the constitution, the laws, and all treaties made or which shall be made under the authority of the United States, shall be the supreme law of the land. A clause in any treaty abolishing slavery would, *ipso facto*, become the supreme law of the land, and there is no power whatever that could interfere with or prevent its operation. By the treaty-making power, any part of the country burdened with slavery, and wrested from us by conquest, could be ceded to a foreign nation who do not tolerate slavery, and without claim of indemnity. The principle is well established that "the release of a territory from the dominion and sovereignty of the country, if that cession be the result of coercion or conquest, does not impose any obligation upon the government to indemnify those who may suffer loss of property by the cession."*

* 1 Kent Com. 178.

The State of New York had granted to her own citizens many titles to real estate lying in that part of her territory now called Vermont. Vermont separated itself from New York, and declared itself an independent State. It maintained its claims to such an extent, that New York, by act of July 14, 1789, was enforced to empower commissioners to assent to its independence; but refused to compensate persons claiming lands under grant from New York, though they were deprived of them by Vermont. The ground taken by the legislature was, that the government was not required to assume the burden of losses produced by conquest or by the violent dismemberment of the State.

Supposing England and France should, by armed intervention, compel the dismemberment of the United States, and the cession of the slave States to them as conquered territory; and that the laws of the conquerors allowed no slaveholding. Could any of the citizens of slave States, who might reside in the free States, having remained loyal, but having lost their slaves, make just legal claim for indemnity upon the government? Certainly not.

Other instances may be cited in which Congress has the power and duty of interference in the local and domestic concerns of States, other than those relating to slavery.* Chief Justice Taney says, —

"Moreover, the constitution of the United States, as far as it has provided for an emergency of this kind, and authorized the general government to interfere in the domestic concerns of a State, has treated the subject as political in its nature, and placed the power in the hands of that department. Art. IV. Sect. 4 of the constitution of the United States provides that the United States shall guarantee to

* *Luther* v. *Borden*, 7 How. 42.

every State in the Union a republican form of government, and shall protect each of them against invasion, and, on the application of the legislature, or of the executive when the legislature cannot be convened, against *domestic violence*. Under this article of the constitution it rests with Congress to decide what government is the established one in a State. For, as the United States guarantees to each State a republican government, Congress must necessarily decide what government is established, before it can determine whether it is republican or not. And when senators and representatives of a State are admitted into the councils of the Union, the authority of the government under which they are appointed, as well as its republican character, is recognized by the proper constitutional authority, and its decision is binding upon every other department of the government, and could not be questioned in a judicial tribunal. So, too, as relates to the clause in the above-mentioned article of the constitution, providing for cases of *domestic* violence. It rested with Congress, too, to determine the means proper to be adopted to fulfil this guaranty."

Suppose, then, that for the purpose of securing "*domestic tranquillity*" and to suppress *domestic violence*, Congress should determine that emancipation of the slaves was a necessary and proper means, it would be the duty of Congress to adopt those means, and thus to interfere with slavery.* If a civil war should arise in a single State between the citizens thereof, it is the duty of Congress to cause *immediate interference* in the domestic and local affairs of that State, and to put an end to the war; and this interference may be by force of arms and by force of laws; and the fact that the cause of quarrel is domestic and private, whether it be in relation to a proposed change in the form of government, as in Dorr's rebellion,* or a rebellion growing out of any other domestic matter, the constitution authorizes and requires interference by the general government. Hence it is obvious that if slaves be considered prop-

* See *Luther* v. *Borden*, 7 How.

erty, and if the regulation of slavery in the States be deemed in some aspects one of the domestic affairs of the States where it is tolerated, yet these facts constitute no reason why such property may not be interfered with, and slavery dealt with by government according to the emergencies of the time, whenever slavery assumes a new aspect, and rises from its private and domestic character to become a matter of national concern, and imperils the safety and preservation of the whole country. We are not to take our opinions as to the extent or limit of the powers contained in the constitution from partisans, or political parties, nor even from the dicta of political judges. We should examine that instrument in the light of history and of reason; but when the language is plain and clear, we need no historical researches to enable us to comprehend its meaning. When the interpretation depends upon technical law, then the contemporary law writers must be consulted. The question as to the meaning of the constitution depends upon what the people, the plain people who adopted it, intended and meant at the time of its adoption.

AUTHORITATIVE CONSTRUCTION OF THE MEANING OF THE CONSTITUTION.

The conclusive authority on its interpretation is the document itself. When questions have arisen under that instrument, upon which the Supreme Court have decided, and one which they had a right to decide, their opinion is, for the time being, the supreme authority, and remains so until their views are changed and new ones announced; and as often as the Supreme Court change their judgments, so often the authoritative interpretation of the constitution changes. The Supreme Court have the right to alter their opinions every time the same question is decided by them; and as new judges must take the place of those whose offices are vacated by death, resignation, or impeachment, it is not unlikely that opinions of the majority of the court may, upon constitutional as well as upon other questions, be sometimes on one side and sometimes on the other.

Upon political discussions, such as were involved in the Dred Scott case, the judges are usually at variance with each other; and the view of the majority will prevail until the majority is shifted. The judges are not legally bound to adhere to their own opinions, although litigants in their courts are. Whenever the majority of the court has reason to overrule a former decision, they not only have the right, but it is their duty, to do so.

The opinions of the framers of the constitution are not authority, but are resorted to for a more perfect understanding of the meaning they intended to convey by the words they used; but after all, the words should speak for themselves; for it was the language in which that instrument was worded that was before the people for discussion and adoption. We must therefore go back to that original source of our supreme law, and regard as of no considerable authority the platforms of political parties who have attempted to import into the constitution powers not authorized by fair interpretation of its meaning, or to deny the existence of those powers which are essential to the perpetuity of the government.

A political party may well waive a legal constitutional right, as matter of equity, comity, or public policy; and this waiver may take the form of a denial of the existence of the power thus waived. In this manner Mr. Douglas not merely waived, but denied, the power of Congress to interfere with slavery in the territories; and in the same way members of the Republican party have disclaimed the right, in time of peace, to interfere with slavery in the States; but such disclaimers, made for reasons of state policy, are not to be regarded as enlarging or diminishing the rights or duties devolved on the departments of government, by a fair and liberal interpretation of all the provisions of the constitution.

Rising above the political platforms, the claims and disclaimers of Federalists, Democrats, Whigs, Republicans, and all other parties, and looking upon the constitution as designed to give the government made by the people, for the people, the powers necessary to its own preservation, and to the enforcement of its laws, it is not possible justly to deny the right of government to interfere with slavery, Mormonism, or any other institution, condition, or social status into which the subjects of the United States can enter, whenever such interference becomes essential as a means of "public welfare or common defence." *

* In several preceding chapters other branches of this subject have been discussed.

INDEX.

CHAPTER I.

CHAPTER II.

CHAPTER III.

CHAPTER IV.

CHAPTER V.

CHAPTER VI.

HAPTER VII.

CHAPTER VIII.

www.ingramcontent.com/pod-product-compliance
Lightning Source LLC
LaVergne TN
LVHW021415110826
845150LV00007B/1930

* 9 7 8 1 4 2 5 5 1 0 4 5 9 *